Pe[illegible] Lucantoni

Cambridge IGCSE®

English as a Second Language

Workbook

Fourth edition

CAMBRIDGE
UNIVERSITY PRESS

CAMBRIDGE
UNIVERSITY PRESS

University Printing House, Cambridge CB2 8BS, United Kingdom

Cambridge University Press is part of the University of Cambridge.

It furthers the University's mission by disseminating knowledge in the pursuit of education, learning and research at the highest international levels of excellence.

www.cambridge.org

First published 2014

Printed in India by Replika Press Pvt. Ltd

ISBN 978-1-107-67202-4

The questions that appear in this book were written by the author and are not actual examination questions.

DEDICATION

Many, many thanks to Lydia Kellas for all her wonderful ideas and interesting suggestions for the activities in this Workbook.

Contents

Menu

PART 1 Leisure and travel		
U1: Focus on reading skills	In this unit, you will: review vocabulary, read about travel and transport, write an article for a travel magazine	Language focus: *whether … or*, introductory phrases with *-ed* or *-ing* words
U2: Focus on reading skills	In this unit, you will: review vocabulary, read about what young people do in their free time, write an explanatory paragraph	Language focus: adjective phrases, adverbs
U3: Focus on writing skills	In this unit, you will: review vocabulary, read about obesity, write a letter/email about healthy eating, write a letter/email to a drinks manufacturer	Language focus: more adjectives and adverbs, *once* and *today*
U4: Focus on listening skills	In this unit, you will: review vocabulary, write about modern transportation	Language focus: prefixes and suffixes, noun forms, tenses
PART 2 Education and work		
U5: Focus on reading skills	In this unit, you will: review vocabulary, read about the risks of playing computer games, write a letter	Language focus: advice phrases, more prefixes and suffixes
U6: Focus on reading and writing skills	In this unit, you will: review vocabulary, read about going to university, write about home-schooling	Language focus: definitions, tenses
U7: Focus on writing and speaking skills	In this unit, you will: review vocabulary, read about 'dirty jobs', write an email applying for a job	Language focus: relative pronouns, comparatives and superlatives, compound nouns
U8: Focus on listening skills	In this unit, you will: review vocabulary, read job advertisements, rewrite a job application	Language focus: reported speech
PART 3 People and achievements		
U9: Focus on reading skills	In this unit, you will: review vocabulary, read about a folk dancer, write numbers, write an article about someone who has achieved something	Language focus: present, present perfect and past tenses
U10: Focus on reading and writing skills	In this unit, you will: review vocabulary, read an article about Felix Baumgartner and write notes to prepare for a talk about him	Language focus: prepositions
U11: Focus on writing skills	In this unit, you will: review vocabulary, read and write about working in Antarctica	Language focus: *either/or*, *neither/nor*, adjectives
U12: Focus on listening skills	In this unit, you will: review vocabulary, read about a scientific study of babies, write a summary	Language focus: 'future in the past', relative pronouns
PART 4 Ideas and the modern world		
U13: Focus on reading skills	In this unit, you will: review vocabulary, read about the effects of the Internet on young people, write an email	Language focus: verb forms
U14: Focus on reading and writing skills	In this unit, you will: review vocabulary, read what young people think about climate change, make notes, write a summary	Language focus: passive verbs, comparisons
U15: Focus on writing skills	In this unit, you will: review vocabulary, read about cookery classes, write an email or letter about taking a cookery class	Language focus: *affect/effect*, adjectives, nouns and verbs
U16: Focus on speaking skills	In this unit, you will: review vocabulary, write about bespoke shoes, write an email about your future career	Language focus: *whether … or*, signpost words, tenses

Introduction

The new edition of this Workbook is for students who are taking the International General Certificate of Secondary Education (IGCSE) in English as a Second Language (E2L) examination, and it has been written to supplement the new edition of the Coursebook.

It is assumed that most of you who use this book will be studying English in order to improve your educational or employment prospects, and it, therefore, includes a broad range of topics and themes relevant to this goal. You will find passages and activities based on a wide variety of stimulating cross-curriculum topics and about people from all over the world, which I hope you will enjoy reading and discussing.

This Workbook follows the same procedure as the Coursebook, with each themed unit focusing on a specific aspect of the IGCSE E2L examination. Furthermore, the Workbook units reinforce areas of language, as well as providing more opportunities for you to research and complete projects. In addition, each unit offers practice in writing skills.

I hope you enjoy using this book!

Peter Lucantoni

Unit 1: Focus on reading skills

A Vocabulary

1 Pair the following words (more than one answer may be possible). Then use the phrases to complete the sentences below.

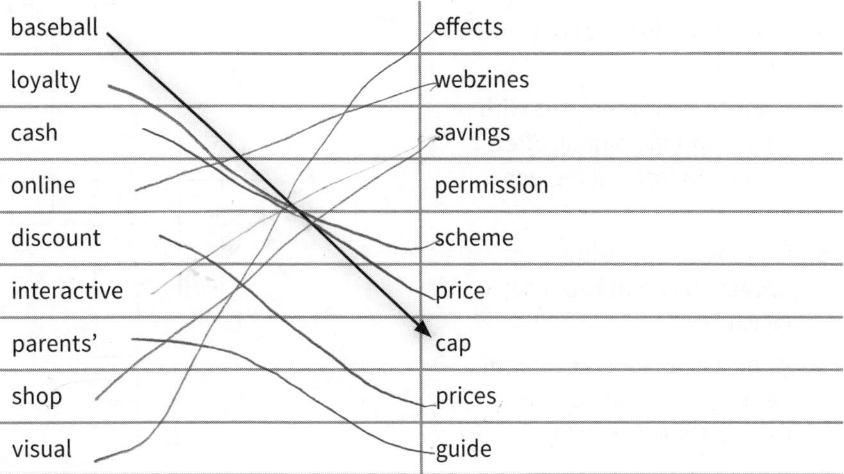

Example: *He was told to remove his baseball cap in the interview.*

a The company is offering a good ________________ to all its new customers to increase sales.

b Large ________________ can be made if you shop at low-cost supermarkets.

c More people are reading ________________ rather than buying the paper version nowadays.

d If products are at a ________________, it is often because they are old or limited stock.

e I found the new bank website very easy to use, as there was a good ________________.

f Children need their ________________ if they are going on the trip.

g ________________ can vary greatly, as often there is no control on what a product costs.

h The ________________ of the new film are brilliant and much better than the old ones.

2 Read the clues and complete the crossword.

Clues

Across

2 An excursion, often in Africa, to see wildlife in its natural habitat (6)

5 Something beautiful and unusual (6)

6 Timetables for a set day and time (9)

7 A dense evergreen area with a high annual rainfall, often located in tropical regions (10)

8 Of a size or splendour suggesting great expense; lavish (9)

10 A sport involving two or four people, who score points using a shuttlecock (9)

12 Something expensive or hard to obtain (6)

Down

1 A meal, often outside, where meat is usually cooked (8)

3 Involving two or more nations (13)

4 A strong, four-wheeled car, originally used in the army (4)

9 A place where tents, huts or other temporary shelters are set up (4)

11 Having or showing great power, skill, strength or force (6)

3 **Look at the words in the table below, which are all used in the text about the Isles of Scilly on page 11. Fill in the gaps. You may not be able to write something in every gap.**

Adjective	Opposite adjective	Noun	Verb	Adverb
beautiful	ugly	beauty		
crumbling				
inhabited				
available				
commercial				
real				
natural				
sparkling				

4 **Think of five more adjectives and add them below the others in the table. Complete the other columns.**

5 **Choose any ten words from your completed table and use them in sentences.**

____

____

____

____

____

____

____

____

____

____

B Use of English

1 **Look at this sentence from the text on page 11:**

Whether you choose to cruise on Scillonian III *or to fly on Skybus … you will be sure to enjoy ….*

Write five sentences of your own to show that you understand how to use the structure *whether … or.*

Example: ***Whether*** *we go on holiday this week or next week, it will cost the same.*

____

____

____

____

____

2 **Look at this sentence from the text on page 9 of your Coursebook:**

This is the one that sold a million in a month.

In the table opposite, write five sentences of your own using the same structure. You can use the words/phrases in the box, but you must make up your own final verb phrase. Copy the table into your notebook if you need more space.

This/That is the …   These/Those are the …

person/people woman/women film/films car/cars team/teams year/years reason/reasons

who when which why that where

Example: *Those are the / reasons / why / he left the country.*

Introductory phase	Noun	Relative pronoun	Verb phrase
This is the	one	that	sold a million in a month.

3 **Look at this phrase from the text on page 16 of your Coursebook:**

Located only minutes from Victoria Falls, the hotel has splendid views …

This information could also be written as:

The hotel is located only minutes from Victoria Falls and has splendid views …

Rewrite the following information, following on from the *-ed* or *-ing* participle.

a *This hotel is regarded as one of the best on the African continent and has been voted the best in Zimbabwe.*

Regarded as ______________________________

____

b *Your evening starts with a meal cooked by our head chef and continues with a programme of African music and dance.*

Starting with ______________________________

____

c *The hotel offers a full range of 5* facilities, including its own cinema, as well as a pool complex with diving boards.*

Offering ______________________________

____

4 Think about your home town, or somewhere that you know well. Write eight sentences about it, using the structures you practised in Activities B2 and B3.

____

____

____

____

____

____

____

____

C Skills

1 Unscramble and rewrite these four pieces of advice on answering questions in Reading and Writing papers.

a sections text search of likely the

____

b question read the

____

c word/s the underline key

____

d question ask asking information yourself the is for what

____

2 Underline the key word or words in each of the questions below.

a How many methods of transport are available to reach the Isles of Scilly?

b What is *Scillonian III*?

c Name four 'treasures' of the islands.

d Which other part of the world are the islands compared with?

e How many people live on the Isles of Scilly?

f What do you need to do before travelling between any of the islands?

g On which island is the Old Wesleyan Chapel?

h Where can you find the second-oldest lighthouse in Britain?

3 Match words from the questions in Activity C2 with the definitions below.

a Small islands.

___

b A small building for Christian worship.

___

c A tower or other tall structure to warn or guide ships at sea.

___

d A quantity of precious metals, gems or other valuable objects.

___

e Name of a place off the south-western coast of Britain.

___

f Something that carries people and objects from one place to another.

___

4 Write down the type of answer that each of the questions in Activity C2 requires.

a *a number (How many … ?)*

b ___

c ___

d ___

e ___

f ___

g ___

h ___

5 Read the text about the Isles of Scilly, then answer the questions from Activity C2.

Discover the Isles of Scilly by air or sea

The Isles of Scilly Steamship Group provides you with two great choices to enjoy a day trip to the islands.

Whether you choose to cruise on *Scillonian III* or to fly on Skybus (the islands' own airline), and whatever time of year you visit, you will be sure to enjoy the natural beauty of the islands.

Exotic plants and wild flowers, ancient cairns and crumbling castles, sparkling white sands and an azure sea – all the treasures of the islands await you. Only 45 kilometres from England's Land's End, but with a real hint of the Tropics.

The Isles are populated by a community of 2000 islanders and there are five inhabited islands to explore to make your day trip one to remember. Inter-island launches are available from St Mary's quay. Check times and tides for availability.

St Mary's, where the airport is situated, is the largest of the islands. Hugh Town, its capital, is the commercial centre and offers a great choice of shops, restaurants and cafés. You will find the Tourist Information Centre at the Old Wesleyan Chapel in Hugh Town. Don't miss the exhibits at the museum or a walk round the Garrison and the Elizabethan fort, now known as the Star Castle Hotel. There are many walks, nature trails and safe white-sand beaches.

The other inhabited islands are St Martin's, Bryher, Tresco and St Agnes. On the latter is a 17th-century lighthouse, the second oldest in Britain, as well as an inn and a café for refreshments. The beaches at Porth Conger and the Cove are great for swimming.

a ___

b ___

c ___

d ___

e ___

f ___

g ___

h ___

Writing

6 Look at these sections of the text. They make the Isles of Scilly sound very attractive.

The Isles of Scilly Steamship Group provides you with two great choices to enjoy a day trip to the islands.

Whether you choose to cruise on Scillonian III *or to fly on Skybus (the islands' own airline), and whatever time of year you visit, you will be sure to enjoy the natural beauty of the islands.*

Re-read the text about the Scilly Isles and underline examples of other words and phrases that make the place sound attractive.

7 Imagine you have been asked to write an article for a travel magazine about a place you know well. Use the Scilly Isles text as a guide for your own piece of writing. Remember – you are 'selling' a place because you want people to visit it, so make it sound attractive. Include the following information:

- name of island/place
- geographical position
- vegetation
- population
- attractive features for tourists
- important towns/places.

Write 100–150 words. Include a map or diagram, and mark places and geographical locations that you have mentioned.

Unit 2: Focus on reading skills

A Vocabulary

1 On page 23 of the Coursebook, you read about holiday activities in Denver. Look at these synonyms for eight adjectives from the text, then write down the adjective. The first letter of each one is given, as well as the number of letters.

a beyond belief, amazing — i n c r e d i b l e

b unchanged — t_ _ _ _ _ _ _

c adored — b_ _ _ _ _ _

d famous, well-known — r_ _ _ _ _ _ _

e sharply defined — a_ _ _ _ _ _

f successful and profitable — b_ _ _ _ _ _

g new and original — c_ _ _ _ _ _ _

h outstandingly good — s_ _ _ _ _ _ _

2 Use the words from Activity A1 to complete these sentences from the text. Then put the sentences in the order in which they appear in the text.

Example: *You'll discover an incredible array of art.*

a The Pepsi Centre is also the home of Denver's ______________ hockey team.

b Catch a performance by the ______________ Colorado Ballet.

c Are you a ______________ teenager? Denver has a ______________ arts world.

d But there's nothing quite like the ______________ thrill of seeing a musical.

e Don't miss the ______________ Denver Art Museum.

f The building itself is a work of art, thanks in part to the amazing, ______________ Hamilton Wing.

3 The words and phrases below are all mentioned in Unit 2. Choose one of the verbs from the box to go before each word or phrase.

watch	do	play	read	help	use

Example: *Do + voluntary work*

a ______________ a hobby.

b ______________ Facebook.

c ______________ sport.

d ______________ voluntary work.

e ______________ computer games.

f ______________ homework.

g ______________ books and magazines.

h ______________ TV.

i ______________ in the home.

j ______________ gardening.

k ______________ a film.

l ______________ a game.

m ______________ the news.

n ______________ the dishwasher.

o ______________ the Internet.

p ______________ an old person.

q ______________ subtitles.

r ______________ a helmet.

s ______________ the message.

4 Choose full expressions from Activity A3 to complete the sentences below. You may need to change the verb form.

Example: *My cousin often* ***plays a game*** *with children at the weekends.*

- **a** I prefer to ______________ on the Internet now and not in newspapers.
- **b** Teenagers should ______________, as adults are often busy working.
- **c** They do not ______________ much at the weekends, as they prefer to go out.
- **d** He spends too much time ______________ and not enough ______________.
- **e** Do you know how to ______________ ? I don't have any idea!
- **f** Teenagers are often made to ______________ at school, as otherwise they wouldn't do any exercise.
- **g** If you ______________ in English on the television, you will improve your vocabulary.
- **h** You should ______________ when you go cycling, to protect your head.

5 Are the following words adjectives, nouns, adverbs or verbs? Put them in the correct column in the table.

activities enormity performance occupy professional increasingly finance usually challenging admission

Adjectives	Nouns	Adverbs	Verbs

6 Use a word from Activity A5 to complete the sentences below. You need to change the form of each word. Say what the new form is.

Example: *The* ***enormous*** *pizza did not fit on the plate and had to be cut into pieces. (adjective)*

- **a** They ______________ the opposing team to another match. (______________)
- **b** The ______________ of the country resulted in great poverty and unhappiness. (______________)
- **c** The children have been asked to ______________ this year, in front of parents and friends. (______________)
- **d** The students were ______________ involved in the lesson by doing it outside the classroom. (______________)
- **e** The ______________ in water consumption is due mostly to wastage. (______________)
- **f** A ______________ consultant was called in to advise the bank. (______________)
- **g** He painted the room very ______________ – it looked amazing! (______________)
- **h** He ______________ to stealing the money and promised to return it immediately. (______________)
- **i** The ______________ method of baking bread is to use yeast. (______________)

B Use of English

1 Underline the adjective phrases in the following sentences. Then write a few words explaining what each adjective phrase means.

Example: *The new museum is* *<u>state-of-the-art</u>* *and attracts many visitors to the town.*
state-of-the-art = modern, advanced

a The argument between the families has been so long-standing that I think they've forgotten what it was about!

____

b The rides at the park are gravity-defying and young children are not allowed on them.

____

c It is much safer to ride your bike off-road, particularly if you are still learning to cycle.

____

d The supermarkets are trying to sell off old stock and are selling many products two-for-one.

____

e She is really hard to please and I find her a very difficult employer.

____

f His driving was pulse-pounding and very dangerous, so I was glad to get out of the car.

____

g The crowds were heart-shaking and I got very frightened, so I went somewhere that was quieter.

____

2 **Use each of the following adjective phrases in a sentence of your own.**

a made of gold

____

b covered in water

____

c cheap but comfortable

____

d eight-page long

____

e double-glazed

____

f black and white

____

g bad-tempered

____

h high-quality

____

3 Unscramble the letters to make adverbs. The first letter is given.

Example: *zaagmyinl* = *amazingly*

a ylefbautiul b______________

b mceployetl c______________

c foulbdytul d______________

d ueaenytllv e______________

e nfbayhisoal f______________

f nsgeeryoul g______________

g nhyguril h______________

h ccorrynietl i______________

4 **Use the words from Activity B3 to complete the sentences.**

Example: ***Amazingly***, *she managed to pass her driving test the first time.*

a The teacher ______________ marked the tests, so they got lower grades.

b They ______________ finished the race after a lot of effort.

c The dog ______________ ate the food.

d They were ______________ surprised by his reaction to their comment.

e She listened to his excuses ______________ , as he always lied.

f He was very ______________ dressed and looked professional.

g All children were asked to give ____________ to the charity.

h She finished off the letter ____________ with her signature.

C Skills

1 How do you spend your free time? How do your parents spend theirs? List four ways that are different and four that are the same in a table like the one below.

Same	Different
We both watch a lot of TV	*I don't read newspapers*

2 You are going to read about a young man called Kelvin Doe, who spent his free time very differently from most young people. Before you read, find eight nouns from the text that are hidden in the word snake.

competitionengineergeneratorimpactscrapspeakersupplytape

3 Read the information opposite about Kelvin Doe, then write down whether you think it is true or false.

a A short film about him has been viewed more than 5 million times on YouTube. ____________

b At 13, he made his own battery. ____________

c At the age of 11, he rummaged in dustbins. ____________

d Doe built a generator. ____________

e He has been featured on CNN and NBC News. ____________

f He presented his inventions to Massachusetts Institute of Technology (MIT) students. ____________

g Kelvin Doe was born in Sierra Leone. ____________

4 In what order do you think the information appears in the text?

____

5 Skim the text and check your answers to Activities C3 and C4. Do not worry about the gaps at the moment.

[1] Kelvin Doe was born in Sierra Leone. Turning 17 this month, he is a good example of how this West African country is trying to rebuild itself and look to the future. Doe is a self-taught **(a)** ____________ of astonishing ability. At the age of 11, he rummaged in dustbins for **(b)** ____________ electronics parts that could fix local problems. At 13, he made his own battery by putting together acid, soda and metal in a tin cup, waiting for the mixture to dry and wrapping **(c)** ____________ around it. Frustrated by the lack of a reliable electricity **(d)** ____________ in his neighbourhood, Doe built a **(e)** ____________, using parts that were home-made or rescued from the rubbish. The generator also powered a community radio station that he built from recycled materials. A short film about him has been viewed more than 5 million times on YouTube.

[2] Kelvin had never been more than 15 kilometres from his home in Freetown until he won a national schools' innovation **(f)** ____________ and was picked last year for a trip to America, where he spoke at the Meet the Young Makers panel at the World Maker Faire in New York. Doe became the youngest ever 'visiting practitioner' with the Massachusetts Institute of Technology (MIT) International Development Initiative. He presented his inventions to MIT students, took part in research and lectured to engineering students at Harvard College. He has been featured on CNN and NBC News and was a **(g)** ____________ at TEDxTeen.

[3] His mentor, David Sengeh, a PhD student at the MIT media lab, said: 'The inspirational effects of the YouTube video have been remarkable. It has had a tremendous **(h)** ____________ on Kelvin's life, on my life and on millions of people all over the world. In Sierra Leone, other young people suddenly feel they can be like Kelvin.'

Adapted from www.theguardian.com

6 Read the text again and fill in the gaps using words from Activity C2.

7 You are going to read another passage from the same article, about a teenage girl, Zea Tongeman. Read the paragraph opposite, then create a second paragraph by matching a phrase from Column A with one from Column B. Put the completed sentences into the correct order.

Zea Tongeman, a 14-year-old from south London, was not a self-proclaimed tech geek. 'I used to think technology was just fixing computers and saying thing like: "Have you tried turning it on and off again?"' But when she realised, after a Little Miss Geek workshop in her school, that tech could be fun and a force for good, she changed her mind. With a friend, Jordan Stirbu, she designed an app called Jazzy Recycling that aims to get people recycling by turning the sometimes tiresome task into a game. Zea comments: 'As Mary Poppins says: "You find the fun and it becomes a game," and that is exactly what our app does.'

Adapted from www.theguardian.com

A	B
1 Jazzy Recycling helps users find places to recycle, tells them what they can recycle	**a** and then enables them to scan, share and get rewards for their efforts.
2 Now Zea has some celebrity backing, and Raj Dhonota,	**b** the game is then shared among friends.
3 She thinks that to have people actually using their app	**c** business consultant and investor, is helping the pair build the app and they hope to launch it very soon.
4 Tapping into the teen mania for sharing even the most mundane titbits of daily life on social media,	**d** and to know that they have made a difference would be incredible.

Writing

8 Which person would you most like to meet: Kelvin or Zea? Write a paragraph of about 80 words, giving your reasons.

Unit 3: Focus on writing skills

A Vocabulary

1 Write a food type for each letter of the alphabet.

A___________________

B___________________

C___________________

D___________________

E___________________

F___________________

G___________________

H___________________

I___________________

J___________________

K___________________

L___________________

M___________________

N___________________

O___________________

P*asta*

Q___________________

R___________________

S___________________

T___________________

U___________________

V___________________

W___________________

X___________________

Y___________________

Z___________________

2 Put the words from Activity A1 into categories. Some words may fit into more than one category.

Fast food	Traditional food	Neither
	Pasta	

3 Use the words in the box to complete the sentences below.

batch cabinet ~~donate~~ neglected registers
sachets sector targets workforce worldwide

Example: *The children were asked to* ***donate*** *some money to the victims of war.*

a The company sets very high ______________ , which are sometimes impossible to achieve.

b Hotels often have ______________ of tea and coffee in the rooms.

c The ______________ was given a day off because of the national holiday.

d Pollution is a ______________ , not a local, problem.

e The animal had been ______________ and needed medical attention.

f You will find everything you need in the ______________ in the bathroom.

g The last ______________ of jam was not as nice as the first one.

h Supermarket checkout ______________ are being replaced by automatic scanners.

i The country is divided up into different parts – each one is called a ______________ .

4 **Add vowels to complete the words.**

a A d _ rty eating ar _ _ can mean a d _ rty kitch _ n.

b A lot of fast food is reh _ _ ted _ ntil it's s _ ld.

c A salad with dr _ ssing is not always the h _ _ lthiest cho _ ce.

d Ask _ ng for '_ xtra' means you have to p _ y more.

e At the end of the n _ ght, food which is not sold is thr _ wn away as r _ bb _ sh.

f The bl _ ck gr _ ll marks on a burg _ r are not from cooking it.

g Workers don't wash th _ _ r hands often en _ _ gh.

h You don't have to _ ccept the food on d _ splay – you c _ n ask for som _ thing to be cooked.

B Use of English

1 **Use words or phrases from each column in the table to make eight opinion phrases.**

I strongly	for	about that
I honestly	imagine	that
I can't	so sure	I'm concerned
I'm not	far as	that
As	my	think
Speaking	point out	experience
Personally,	believe	myself
I'd like to	I	with that
In	don't agree	

Example: *I strongly believe that …*

a ______________________________

b ______________________________

c ______________________________

d ______________________________

e ______________________________

f ______________________________

g ______________________________

h ______________________________

2 **Use each phrase you came up with in Activity B1 in a complete sentence.**

Example: *I strongly believe that people should be warned about the dangers of eating fast food.*

a ____________________

b ____________________

c ____________________

d ____________________

e ____________________

f ____________________

g ____________________

h ____________________

3 **In the following dialogue, two people are giving their opinions about fast food and traditional cooking. Underline the phrases used to express an opinion, then put the dialogue in the correct order. One has been done as an example.**

a 'I'd like to point out that she does not see it as "tied", because she loves cooking.'

b 'As far as I'm concerned, the best food in the world is cooked by my mum.'

c 'I can't imagine how much time she spends in the kitchen, tied to the saucepans.'

d 'Personally, I think you can get some really great fast food.'

e 'In my experience, it depends who's cooking it. And I'd like to point out that not everyone is a good cook.'

f 'I'm not so sure about that. She could be doing something else.'

g 'Speaking for myself, I'd rather eat at home any day. At least then I know what I'm eating.'

h 'I honestly don't agree with that, but you must agree that home cooking tastes much better.'

1 b___ 2 ___ 3 ___ 4 ___

5 ___ 6 ___ 7 ___ 8 ___

4 **The following two phrases are taken from the *Shellfish in Oman* text on page 40 of your Coursebook. Look at how the adverbs *once* and *today* are used:**

Once, *abalone shellfish were brought to the surface ...*

Today, *the shellfish are caught for ...*

Here, *once* means 'at some time in the past', and *today* means 'at the present time'.

Think of two other ways to say *once* and *today*. Then write three sentences for 'at some time in the past' and three sentences for 'at the present time' using the phrases.

'at some stage in the past'	'at the present time'
once	today

'at some stage in the past'

a ____________________

b ____________________

c ____________________

'at the present time'

d ____________________

e ____________________

f ____________________

5 **Look at this sentence that includes the phrase *in addition to*:**

Vegans, in addition to being vegetarian, do not use other animal products.

We use *in addition to* to give more information, or to join two or more pieces of information. It can come at the start of a sentence or within it.

Examples: *People choose to be vegan for health, environmental and/or ethical reasons.*

*People choose to be vegan for health reasons, **in addition to** environmental and/or ethical reasons.*

*People who choose to be vegan do so for environmental and/or ethical reasons, **in addition to** health reasons.*

In your notebooks, rewrite the following information using *in addition to*.

a A healthy and varied vegan diet includes fruits, vegetables and plenty of leafy greens, as well as wholegrain products, nuts, seeds and legumes.

b Vegan diets are free of cholesterol and are generally low in fat.

c Calcium is found in dark-green vegetables and many other foods commonly eaten by vegans.

d *Simply Vegan* contains a complete discussion of vegan nutrition, plus 160 quick and easy recipes.

C Skills

1 **You are going to read a text about obesity. First, look at these questions and make some brief notes. Use a dictionary to help you.**

a What does obesity mean?

____

b What do you think causes obesity?

____

c In which countries do most people suffer from obesity? Why?

____

d Do you think the levels of obesity are changing? Why?

____

2 **Read the text opposite and choose a heading from the box for each paragraph.**

Class and trends
Health dangers of obesity
Statistics on the sales of fattening foods
Not just what you eat
Shoppers' habits
Sales of healthier products

Obesity – fat of the land

Governments are under pressure to change the way people eat, although it already seems that diets are changing. Unfortunately, there is more resistance with younger consumers, as peer pressure tends to have more impact than any amount of government intervention. Given mankind's need to worry, it is not surprising that the diseases of prosperity – stress, depression and, increasingly, obesity – get a lot of attention.

(a) ________________________________

Obesity is a serious problem, as it increases the risk of diabetes, heart disease and cancer and is the fifth leading risk for global deaths. From 2008, 1.4 billion adults were overweight; that refers to adults who are 20 and older and is 10% of the world's population. It is not clear what governments can do about it, and evidence suggests that the idea of imposing taxes on foods is not necessarily the answer. In Sweden, where advertising to young people is already banned, children are as overweight as they are in any comparable country. In fact, in 2011, more than 40 million children under the age of five were overweight worldwide.

(b) ________________________________

But, despite the statistics, there is an obvious change that is happening worldwide. Shoppers' behaviour suggests that an opposite trend is developing. It is not just the flight from carbohydrates; there is a broader shift going on.

(c) ________________________________

Companies are edging away from fattening foods. Five years ago, chocolate made up 80% of sales in a world-leading company; now, that is down to half. Five years ago, 85% of drinks sales were sweet, fizzy stuff. That's down to 56%. The rest is mostly juice. Diet drinks – which make up a third of the sales of fizzy drinks – are growing at 5% a year, while sales of the fattening stuff are static.

(d) ________________________________

Supermarkets say that people are buying healthier foods. Lower-calorie ranges grew by 12% in 2003: twice the growth in overall sales. Sales of fruit and vegetables are growing faster than overall sales too. Cafés and restaurants also report an increase in healthy eating. A sandwich store says that sales of salads grew by 63% last year.

(e) ________________________________

But it isn't just eating too much fatty stuff that makes people fat. It's laziness too. That may be changing. According to a market-research company, there were 3.8 million members of private gyms last year, up from 2.2 million in 1998. The average man got thinner in 2002.

(f) ________________________________

Obesity is also seen as a class issue, with more than 30 million overweight children living in developing countries and 10 million in developed countries.

Source: *The Economist*.

3 **Read the article again and answer the questions.**

a Who has more influence on what young people eat?

b In Sweden, what is forbidden and what is the result?

c What suggests that there is a change occurring?

d What are listed as the main culprits of weight gain?

e Give **at least three** examples of changes in people's eating habits.

f How do we know that obesity is more of an issue with certain groups of people?

Writing

4 **You want to start a campaign at your school to raise awareness of healthy eating. You have written to some major companies in the food industry to get information about the contents of their food products. In your notebook, write a letter/email telling your headteacher about your enquiries. In your letter, you should explain:**

- who you wrote to and the focus of your enquiries
- what you are planning to do with the information
- the advantages you think your campaign might bring to the school.

Your letter/email should be 150–200 words long (Extended) or 100–150 words long (Core).

5 **You want to contact a major drinks company whose products you think are bad for young people's health. In your notebook, write a letter to the company, explaining why you are against them producing and selling these drinks to young people. In your letter, you should explain:**

- who you are and the reason you are writing
- why you think the company should not be promoting and selling its drinks
- the kind of drinks you think should be produced and sold.

Your letter/email should be 150–200 words long (Extended) or 100–150 words long (Core).

Unit 4: Focus on listening skills

A Vocabulary

1 Find **12** forms of transportation in the wordsearch.

D	A	T	W	O	B	V	C	I	E	S	U	H	I	T
C	F	R	S	U	B	M	A	R	I	N	E	C	R	U
R	U	M	O	F	H	W	E	S	G	O	Z	A	H	N
U	N	V	P	T	W	S	R	N	A	Y	M	B	N	T
I	S	R	N	M	O	T	O	R	B	I	K	E	O	I
S	A	G	H	Y	C	X	P	V	S	D	J	A	O	K
E	J	O	L	N	S	I	L	A	S	E	O	R	L	S
L	W	K	G	I	Q	Y	A	G	B	N	L	I	L	S
I	M	A	U	H	D	I	N	R	Z	R	B	C	A	I
N	J	Y	T	S	H	E	E	A	I	F	L	K	B	U
E	R	A	B	E	W	I	R	P	Q	T	R	S	P	Y
R	A	K	M	C	U	L	E	M	X	D	R	H	S	W
P	M	O	N	O	R	A	I	L	D	I	N	A	R	Q
Y	V	W	E	L	C	Y	C	I	B	Y	V	W	I	D
L	I	B	A	D	D	R	E	V	M	G	O	E	R	N

2 Put the words from the wordsearch in the correct category. There are three words for each category.

Air transport	Rail transport	Maritime transport	Road transport
balloon			

3 Look at the phrases below, which come from texts in your Coursebook. What do the underlined words and phrases mean? Rewrite them in your own words.

Example: *Since they <u>appeared</u> on the streets of Uganda …*
Since they were first seen …

a Turkey is <u>awash</u> with ancient cities.

____

b Modern-day Turkey covers an area that has stood at the <u>crossroads of history</u>.

____

c … whether it's a relaxing beach holiday, a <u>city-break</u> or a journey into the country's …

____

d Give space on the left, and don't <u>hug the kerb</u> if a car behind you gets impatient.

____

e Make <u>eye contact</u> with drivers.

____

f Other initiatives are also <u>springing up</u>.

____

g … the <u>strain</u> that road fatalities could have on the economy is worrying politicians.

____

h … <u>monopolising</u> hospital budgets.

____

4 Look at the following sentences that include the word *book*.

Well, of course, we had ***booked*** *everything well in advance.*

Answer the questions in your ***book****.*

Write sentences to show the difference in meaning between the following pairs of words.

a mourning / morning

____

____

b key (words) / key (lock)

____

____

c weather / whether

____

____

d new / knew

____

____

e weak / week

____

____

f watch (see) / watch (time)

____

____

5 **Choose which form of transportation is being described.**

bus car motorbike balloon train ferry bicycle coach campervan taxi quadbike

a It travels on water and carries people and goods, as well as vehicles.

____

b Many people drive one of these as their own personal form of transport.

____

c A home on wheels. __________

d It has two wheels and normally only carries one person. __________

e It travels long distances by road, carrying large numbers of passengers.

____

f Not normally used as a form of aviation transport, but often used for entertainment. __________

g Normally transports people in a town, or short distances outside a town.

____

h Has two wheels and an engine and is normally used to transport one person. __________

i Can cover long distances quickly and efficiently with many passengers.

____

j It has four wheels and is not a common form of transport.

____

k The passenger normally pays for each journey they take. __________

B Use of English

1 **Change the following verbs into nouns, using the suffix -*ation*.**

a accelerate __________

b industrialise __________

c transport __________

d populate __________

e decelerate ______________

f inflame ______________

g irritate ______________

h concentrate ______________

i mobilise ______________

j manipulate ______________

k stimulate ______________

2 Now write the words in alphabetical order.

acceleration

______________ ______________

______________ ______________

______________ ______________

______________ ______________

______________ ______________

3 Many words can have two noun forms. Look at the list of verbs and nouns in Activity B1, then write another noun next to the first one you thought of.

Example: *accelerate (verb)* *acceleration (action)* *accelerator (thing)*

4 Complete the following sentences using words from the activities in this section.

a The new model of the car had excellent ______________ compared to the old one.

b Touching the plant can ______________ some people's skin, so take care.

c There was massive ______________ of people from the area because of the storm warning.

d If you learn to ______________ harder in exams, you should get a better grade.

e The ______________ of the world has increased dramatically.

f You should ______________ more quickly at a roundabout.

g The country started to ______________ in the 19th century.

h The ______________ on her skin got worse, so she needed antibiotics.

i If you ______________ somebody, then you are taking advantage of them.

j They needed to ______________ his heart after the attack.

k The country's ______________ system has much improved recently.

5 The words *antibiotics* and *transportation* begin with prefixes: *anti-* and *trans-*. Match the prefixes with the correct meaning.

pre-	with, jointly, completely
im-	one
ex-	before
trans-	opposing, against, the opposite
re-	into, on, near, towards
anti-	across, beyond
com-	out of, away from
mono-	air, atmosphere, aviation
aero-	back, again

6 Write two more words in your notebook that begin with each of the prefixes in Activity B5.

7 Match the sentences on page 27 with one of the tenses from the box.

'will' future	present continuous
past simple	present perfect simple

a The boys are playing football outside again in the field. ______________________

b They always played in the school grounds before they locked the gates. ______________

c They have never travelled on a train before.

____

d They will probably visit their grandparents this afternoon. ______________________

8 Complete the sentence by writing in the verbs in the correct tense.

a He ____________ (*buy*) a new bicycle yesterday and he ____________ (*already damage*) it!

b I ____________ (*do*) my English homework tonight and maths tomorrow.

c They ____________ (*have*) breakfast at the moment, so please call later.

d She ____________ (*put up*) her umbrella because it just ____________ (*start*) to rain.

e I just ____________ (*eat*), so I do not want anything, thank you.

f My friend ____________ (*move*) to Canada one year ago, so he ____________ (*be*) there since January.

g Tomorrow I think I ____________ (*start*) my new project.

h I ____________ (*finish*) it by the end of the month.

9 Fill in the answer in the correct tense from the choices below each sentence.

a Who ____________ the food last night when your mother was working?

i) cooks ii) is cooking iii) has been cooking iv) cooked

b Where is Anthony? He ____________ his car in the garage.

i) repairs ii) is repairing iii) has repaired iv) repaired

c I love this film. I ____________ it two or three times already.

i) see ii) have seen iii) had seen iv) saw

d Have you visited any other Asian countries?

Yes, I ____________ Vietnam two years ago.

i) visited ii) have visited iii) had visited iv) will visit

e She ____________ the living room if you want her.

i) has cleaned ii) has been cleaning iii) is cleaning iv) will clean

f This time tomorrow I ____________ on a beach.

i) will be sunbathing ii) will sunbathe iii) will have sunbathed iv) sunbathed

g You arrived two days ago and already you ____________ all your money!

i) spend ii) have spent iii) will spend iv) are spending

C Skills

1 **Read this tip about Listening exams and fill in the gaps with the correct words.**

In Listening exams, you will hear everything **(a)** ______________. You should concentrate all the time and make **(b)** ______________ of **(c)** ______________ words to help you. A good **(d)** ______________ is to use the second time you listen to check your **(e)** ______________ from the first time.

Writing

2 **Your school is having a writing competition. The title of the competition is *The impact of modern transportation on our society.***

Write your entry for the competition, expressing your opinion and using the ideas and vocabulary from this unit to help you.

Your entry should be about 150–200 words long (Extended) or 100–150 words long (Core).

Unit 5: Focus on reading skills

A Vocabulary

1 **Put the italic letter groups into the correct words from Unit 5 in your Coursebook. There is one example.**

are	l _ _ n	*en*	intol _ _ _ nt	pol _ _ y
_ _ unselling	~~*ten*~~	ex***ten***sive	*oa*	bl _ _ ded
um	*ic*	*ria*	*era*	*ate*
vol _ _ es	welf _ _ _	*co*	self-c _ _ _ ring	approp _ _ _ te

2 **Use the words from Activity A1 to complete the following sentences.**

Example: ***Extensive*** *research was done into the benefits of salt in the diet.*

a It is now the school's ______________ that all students wear school uniform.

b We guarantee that the ______________ of the children is of the upmost importance.

c The library books are out on ______________ , so you cannot borrow them for now.

d The holiday flats were ______________ and much cheaper than a hotel.

e It is not ______________ to use your mobile phone in a meeting or lesson.

f They offered ______________ to the children who had seen the accident.

g When the two paints were ______________ , they produced an entirely different colour.

h They bought all the ______________ of the new series when it was published.

i They are very ______________ of other people.

3 **Look at the following word groups from Unit 5 of your Coursebook. In each group, one of the words has been misspelt. Underline the word and rewrite it correctly.**

Example: *facilities* *illustrating* <u>*referance*</u> ***reference***

a leisure programme acommodation ______________

b cafetaria counselling timetabled ______________

c pronunciation grammer examination ______________

d	libarian	appropriate	vegetarian	______________
e	examination	referance	beginner	______________
f	counsellor	purchase	teenages	______________
g	alternative	problem	enviroment	______________

4 Write down which of the words from Activity A3b each of the following sentences is describing.

Example: *Somebody who does not eat meat.* ***Vegetarian***

a A person who works with books. ______________

b A service that may help people who are having problems or who need advice. ______________

c A test to show a person's progress, knowledge or ability. ______________

d The set of rules that explain how words are used in a language. ______________

e Somewhere you can buy and eat food. ______________

f The natural world. ______________

g Offering or expressing a choice. ______________

5 Make complete sentences by matching phrases from each column.

1 Evidence is emerging that teenagers …	**a** … wide range of graded reading books.
2 It is important in some exam questions …	**b** … various skills.
3 In most writing exams, you need to show …	**c** … are biologically incapable of going to bed at a sensible time.
4 Students can choose from a very …	**d** … to show that you can understand information presented in a visual format.
5 We have special software to help you practise …	**e** … and *advise* (verb) are often confused.
6 The words *advice* (noun) …	**f** … different verb tenses or parts of verbs, adjectives or adverbs.
7 In a speaking exam, you should …	**g** … that you can write in both a formal and an informal style.
8 A prefix is a group of letters added …	**h** … before a word or base to change its meaning.
9 Different suffixes can change words into nouns, …	**i** … try to use a variety of structures and vocabulary.

1 c ______________	**4** ______________	**7** ______________
2 ______________	**5** ______________	**8** ______________
3 ______________	**6** ______________	**9** ______________

B Use of English

1 Look at the following sentences. Underline the advice phrases.

- **a** If I were you, I'd visit the doctor soon to check that cough.
- **b** I think it would be better if you came later, as I won't be ready.
- **c** It might be a good idea to read the book before seeing the film.
- **d** Why don't we take the dog for a walk now, before it rains?
- **e** I don't think she should buy that car, as it's too expensive.

2 Which expressions in Activity B1 are followed by *to*? Underline them. Which expressions are followed by an infinitive without *to*? Double underline them.

3 Use numbers to indicate the correct order for the dialogue below.

Merlin: Yes, I think it would be better to go in the summer, as it'll be freezing now.
Merlin: **Are you coming on the school trip next week? [1]**
Merlin: Umm … I don't think you should, as they're always rushing around at that time.
Merlin: Yes, that would be better and I think you should tell them, as they like you …
Merlin: Yes, that's not a bad idea, but I think we should tell them soon.

Yvonne: What about during the break then?
Yvonne: Why don't we tell that to the teachers?
Yvonne: If I were you, I'd tell them tomorrow morning before classes start.
Yvonne: Yes, I'm thinking about it, but it's in the mountains and will be cold.

4 Complete the sentences using the word stems in brackets. For each word, you need to add a prefix from the box and put the verb into the correct tense.

mis-	un-	re-	over-	dis-	trans-
be-	co-	de-	fore-	~~pre~~-	

Example: *Can you … the answer to this question? (-dict)*

Can you pre + dict the answer to this question?

- **a** The dog tried to ______________ the boy in the park. (*-friend*)
- **b** Because she ______________ the instructions, she did the activity incorrectly. (*-understand*)
- **c** The exercise was ______________ and so she finished it quickly. (*-complicate*)
- **d** They wanted to ______________ the area, as it was so beautiful. (*-visit*)
- **e** He missed the bus because he ______________ again after a late night. (*-sleep*)
- **f** She looked at him in ______________ because of the lies he was telling. (*-belief*)
- **g** If you ______________ better, then you will finish the project quickly. (*-operate*)
- **h** Because the country's currency was ______________, prices rose drastically. (*-value*)
- **i** She was ______________ when she had her hair restyled. (*-form*)
- **j** They did not ______________ that the house would be destroyed during the hurricane. (*-see*)

5 Complete the crossword using the words from Activity B4.

Clues

Across

2 Completely change (9)
4 Refusal or reluctance to trust (9)
7 Simple (13)
9 Predict or know in advance (7)
10 Become someone's friend (8)

Down

1 Go to a place again (7)
3 Sleep for longer than you should (9)
5 Get something wrong (13)
6 Work with others (9)
8 Reduce or cancel the value of something (7)

6 Underline the suffix in each word.

Example: *happiness*

a accidental
b availability
c cheaper
d excitement
e guidance
f happiness
g imagination
h luxuriously
i loving

7 The following sentences sound strange! Rewrite the sentences, turning each of the underlined phrases into a word with a suffix.

Example: *David painted the picture with great care.*
David painted the picture carefully.

a Antoinette paints without caring.

____

b I wrote a letter full of gratitude for the lovely flowers.

____

c They saw a puppy without a home wandering the streets.

____

d That painting is full of beauty.

____

e Big dogs, if well looked after, are without harm.

____

f Did you see the houses full of colour in that street?

____

g The car is without worth now that it has been damaged.

____

h The computer is no use because it is so old.

____

C Skills

1 Read the article and choose which phrase from the box belongs in which gap.

can be so extreme	do physical damage	for hours on end
gaming addiction	in poor physical condition	
more likely to suffer	infested with hostile creatures	
on the verge of	to eat properly	

What's the danger for video-game players?

You've been searching all day. You've travelled hundreds of kilometres, sometimes backtracking to make sure you haven't missed anything. Some areas are so **(a)** ______________ that you've been prevented from continuing on your journey until the creatures were destroyed. After all that, you've finally found what you've been looking for: the secret passage that transports you to another place: you've moved up to the next level! You've done it! You're so excited that you barely notice how much your back hurts, youdon't notice that you are **(b)** ______________ getting a migraine headache again, nor do you realise that you haven't had anything to eat or drink all day.

It may sound like a strange story, but it's all too familiar for video-game players. Whether they play on an Xbox or online, they enter worlds filled with strange creatures by travelling to mysterious and sometimes secret locations. They spend so much time in this other world that they could begin to **(c)** ______________ to their bodies. Physical consequences of gaming addiction include carpal tunnel, migraines, backaches, eating irregularities, among other things.

Carpal Tunnel Syndrome (CTS)

CTS has long been associated with computer use, so it's no surprise that it's a physical symptom of **(d)** ______________. CTS is caused when the main nerve between the forearm and the hand is squeezed or pressed. This occurs when the carpal tunnel (the part of the wrist where the main nerve and tendons are located) becomes irritated or swollen. Overuse of a computer mouse can cause such irritation and swelling, as can excessive use of a video-game controller.

Migraines

Migraine headaches typically start in one spot and slowly spread, getting more painful as they progress. In severe cases, the pain **(e)** ______________ that it causes the sufferer to vomit. Both light and noise can cause excessive pain. Someone who plays video games for extended periods of time is **(f)** ______________ from migraines because of the intense concentration required and the strain put on the eyes.

Backaches

Backaches are a common physical symptom of gaming addiction because most gamers stay seated in the same position **(g)** ______________. The lack of movement causes stiffness and soreness, but could deteriorate into chronic back problems over a longer period of time.

Eating irregularities

Eating irregularities are caused by gaming addiction simply because most addicted gamers don't want to take the time **(h)** ______________. Rather than eating healthy, balanced meals, they eat food that is quick and usually unhealthy. In extreme cases, the gamer may choose not to eat at all.

These physical consequences may occur in varying degrees from one gamer to another and, of course, if a gamer is already **(i)** ______________, they will be more susceptible to these effects.

Adapted from www.video-game-addiction.org

2 Answer these questions about the text.

a What might prevent a gamer from continuing on their journey?

____

b Where might you go after finding the secret passage?

____

c Being excited means a gamer may not notice **three** things. What are they?

____

d Why can overuse of a computer mouse cause CTS?

____

e What might the physical effect be of intense concentration and eye strain?

____

f When could a chronic back problem occur?

____

g Why do many gamers eat unhealthy food?

____

h Which type of gamer is more likely to suffer physically?

____

Writing

3 You have seen the announcement opposite on posters in your town and school.

'Save our playing field' campaign

Parents complain about us sitting all day at the computer!
Now they are threatening to sell the playing field next to our school!
It is the only safe place nearby where we can play sports.
In the summer, the field is used for festivals and the popular 'world music' concert.
Developers want to build a new shopping centre there.

Don't let this happen!

Write to your local newspaper expressing your opinions about the importance of OUR playing field.

Find out more: www.noshops.eur

Write a letter to a friend:

- giving reasons why the playing field should be saved
- saying why your community needs the playing field
- giving alternative suggestions for the site of the new shopping centre.

Your letter should be 150–200 words long (Extended) or 100–150 words long (Core).

Unit 6: Focus on reading and writing skills

A Vocabulary

1 The notes opposite each describe one of the jobs in the box below. Rewrite the notes by completing the words and making full sentences. Then identify which job is being described.

surgeon	teacher
~~pilot~~	engineer
policeman	

Example: *Works shift hrs & travels 2 many diff countries.*

This person works shift hours and travels to many different countries. ***Pilot***

a Many yrs at uni r nec 2 do job which can b v challeng and demand. They play a v import role in our society in looking after people & mak them well.

____

____

b Again uni ed is v imp for this job. They play a v imp role in our develop as an adult & we learn many interesting thngs from them.

____

____

c Maintain peace & secur in our cities and wear unif so that can b easily identif. Men & w/men are both nec in this job.

____

____

d Do many diff jobs in the build and construct of city. Again a uni degr is extrem imp as there are so many areas 2 learn about.

____

____

2 Underline the key words that helped you identify the job.

Example: *This person works shift hours and <u>travels to many different countries</u>.*

3 Look at these examples of 'signpost' words:

In addition*, with each issue we provide you with a list of online links.*

… many of which ***also*** *have MP3 audio files …*

Complete the sentences using the signpost words in the box.

also	in addition	finally	moreover	during	furthermore
besides	consequently	whenever	sometimes	while	

a The job of a teacher, __________ it can be very satisfying, can __________ be very challenging.

b __________ your career, you need to continue learning __________ to teaching, if you want to develop as a professional.

c __________ you are expected to fulfil requirements from your bosses __________ those of your class.

d ______________ the workload can become quite stressful and ______________ performance can be affected.

e But a good teacher is a dedicated one and ______________ one who loves their job.

f ______________, a teacher is a person who ______________ asked will give.

in this case	namely
consequently	in other words
in spite of	specifically
for this reason	such as
however	for example
as a result	accordingly

4 Put the signpost words from the box on the left into the correct category in the table. There are two for each category.

Make clear	Contrast/ difference	Detail	Result/ consequence	Example	Summary

5 Complete the sentences using one of the words/phrases from Activity A4.

a I told you I'm not going, ______________ 'I'm staying here'.

b They painted the house, but more ______________ the upstairs rooms.

c They say they don't go out much, ______________ being out every weekend.

d We've been told to bring lunch, ______________ a sandwich and a drink.

e He got a pay rise and ______________ they are going on holiday next month.

f We normally ask for a letter from your parents, but ______________ we'll make an exception.

g They've spent all their money and ______________ they are not going shopping tomorrow.

h They love trying out different restaurants, ______________ the new ones in town.

B Use of English

1 Beneath each of the sentences on page 37, write a brief definition of the underlined phrase.

Example: *Get involved with social networking sites.*

Places on the Internet where you can meet people and make contacts.

a Many young people end up taking a traditional path in life and follow their parents.

___

b Potential employers are looking for candidates who show inventiveness.

___

c If you strike up a relationship at the beginning with your colleagues, then you will enjoy the job more.

___

d You could land your first assignment early, if the management is impressed with your performance.

___

e He dresses in a very old-fashioned, but charming, way.

___

f You should do a course that best fits your interests.

___

2 Circle the word or phrase that correctly completes each sentence.

a Preparing with your teacher for an interview practises what … in a live situation.

i) will experience ii) experienced

iii) will be experienced

b When working in a new job you should be prepared … to do anything.

i) to be asked ii) to ask iii) asked

c Are they … some treats in their lunch box?

i) allow to include ii) including

iii) allowed to include

d They … not to go out tonight because they've got exams tomorrow.

i) were asked ii) had been asked

iii) have been asked

e She … to do a trial period before she is given the job permanently.

i) might expect ii) might be expected

iii) expected

f She has been … give three references for the job.

i) asked to ii) asked iii) asking

g Why do you think their decision was … on that fact?

i) based on ii) dependent iii) based

h This is a major international company … the others you've applied to.

i) as ii) compared iii) compared to

i You talk about doing voluntary work. Which … are you referring to?

i) topics ii) volunteer iii) type

j If you are looking for work you should … the Internet in your search.

i) exclude ii) involve iii) include

3 Unscramble the following words to make complete sentences. Say which tense is being used.

Example: *claustrophobia I've feelings had of no*

I've had no feelings of claustrophobia.
Present perfect.

a doorbell he down just sat dinner when had the to rang

___

b evening they day in work eat every the after

___

c started they when home walking it to were rain

___

d Australia I've love to and never would to been visit

___

e house they to will the come later

___

f some they need milk we bought, so don't any more yesterday

____

g for have ages these coming they to classes been

____

h years of built were ago hundreds they

____

C Skills

1 The following words and phrases appear in the text opposite. Match them to the correct definition. Use a dictionary to help you understand any unknown words.

contribute short salary graduate academic reputation initially depend expenses

a connected to education ____________________

b money you earn ____________________

c not enough ____________________

d costs ____________________

e to begin with ____________________

f add ____________________

g good name ____________________

h person who has a university degree

____

i rely ____________________

2 The title of the text is *I was concerned I would be left out*. What do you think the speaker meant by *left out* here?

a on my own

b left alone

c not included in a group

3 Skim the text and check whether your answer to Activity C2 is correct.

I was concerned I would be left out

Bimla knew that she wanted to go to university when she got her IGCSE results. But she had been worried that she would not be accepted by the other students once she got there.

Although she had always been told at her school that she would do well at university, she nonetheless believed that other students would be better than her. 'I know I got good grades at school, but I thought that they wouldn't be enough and that I would be left out by the other students,' she admits. Some of her friends thought she shouldn't even think about going to university, but she didn't agree with that and said, 'I think university should be for everyone, no matter where they come from or what their background is.'

Growing up in a large family, she'd always understood that her parents would depend on the children to contribute money to the home. 'We all knew we'd have to help pay the expenses at home, so when I told my parents I wanted to do my IGCSEs before going to university, they weren't very pleased initially,' she recalls. 'But soon they accepted the idea when they thought about the advantages of having a university graduate in the family.'

Money was short at home, so Bimla worked after her IGCSEs and saved nearly everything from her salary. She wanted to work in medicine, so she looked around and found a university near home, which meant she could stay at home and study at the same time.

The university had a good academic reputation and she thought she wouldn't get in, so she was very excited when she was offered a place. 'I never thought it possible,' she admits.

Three years later and she remembers her fears of being left out. 'I've made some really great friends and everybody has been so helpful, even the lecturers! The idea that you are not good enough because you are different is so wrong – university is not like that.'

She wants to say to other families, 'If your child is good enough and really wants to go on to university, then you can't imagine the advantages there will be for you and your family.'

4 Find and underline the vocabulary from Activity C1 in the text.

5 Answer these questions.

a When did Bimla know that she wanted to go to university?

____

b What worried Bimla about going to university?

____

c What does Bimla mean when she says that university should be for everyone?

____

d What did Bimla's parents expect their children to do?

____

e Why did Bimla's parents change their minds about her doing IGCSEs before university?

____

f What was the advantage in finding a university near her home?

____

g Why did Bimla think she would not be accepted by the university?

____

6 Imagine that you have been educated at home rather than in school. You now want to go to university, as Bimla did. What do you think would be your strengths and weaknesses at university? Use a table like the one below.

	Strengths	Weaknesses
Socialising		
Applying yourself to a structured education		
Dealing with external deadlines and pressures		
Style of work demanded by the university		
Style of work demanded by the university		

Writing

7 Use the information in the table you completed in Activity C6 to write a description of what you think your strengths and weaknesses would be at university if you had been home-schooled. Your description should be 150–200 words long (Extended) or 100–150 words long (Core).

Unit 7: Focus on writing and speaking skills

A Vocabulary

1 In Unit 7 of the Coursebook, you saw the words *impression* and *professional*. Use the table below to make more words that are spelt with *-ss-*. Join letters from column A with letters from column B, using *-ss-* in the middle.

A		B
a		ue
ba		ette
pa		*ertion*
ca		oon
me	*-ss-*	ive
ma		port
ti		age
succe		enger
pa		ful

a *a + ss + ertion = assertion*

b ______________________

c ______________________

d ______________________

e ______________________

f ______________________

g ______________________

h ______________________

i ______________________

2 Match the words from Activity A1 to a definition below.

a paper handkerchief ______________________

b very large ______________________

c person who is transported in a vehicle ______________________

d something you strongly believe ______________________

e official document you must travel with ______________________

f doing well ______________________

g magnetic tape ______________________

h information given to someone ______________________

i large woodwind instrument ______________________

3 Use the secret code to find words from Unit 7 in the grid below. What name is hidden in the vertical column?

1	2	3	4	5	6	7	8	9	10	11	12	13
a	b	c	d	e	f	g	h	i	j	k	l	m

14	15	16	17	18	19	20	21	22	23	24	25	26
n	o	p	q	r	s	t	u	v	w	x	y	z

Example: 2 5 3 1 21 19 5 = because

					2	5	**3**	1	21	19	5				because
					4	9	**1**	12	15	7	21	5			
			16	1	22	5	**13**	5	14	20					
					6	9	**2**	5	18						
		12	1	2	15	21	**18**								
						19	**9**	4	5	23	1	12	11		
							4	5	6	5	14	3	5		
		21	14	4	5	18	**7**	18	15	21	14	4			
					6	21	**5**	12	12	5	4				

____

4 Below are some of the most commonly misspelt words in the English language. Write the correct spellings next to each word. In the third column, write the words in alphabetical order.

independant ______________ ______________

definate ______________ ______________

concience ______________ ______________

mischievious	____________	____________	changable	____________	____________
accomadate	____________	____________	maintenunce	____________	____________
existance	____________	____________	hierarche	____________	____________
calender	____________	____________	exhilerate	____________	____________
indispensible	____________	____________	alphabeticle	____________	____________
disciplane	____________	____________	noticable	____________	____________
lisense	____________	____________	beleive	____________	____________

B Use of English

1 Look at these sentences using relative pronouns:

I am a student ***who*** *is studying English.*

The good talkers, ***whom*** *you admire, know these rules.*

Write complete sentences using the correct relative pronoun. You will need to use some pronouns more than once.

There is a film on at the cinema	who	people play tennis.
A fireman is a person		they got married?
Is this the article in the newspaper	which	I would like to see.
Do you know the reason	that	he left the room so quickly?
Do you think they would forget the day		makes things with his hands.
A cathedral is a place	where	passed all her exams.
That was the girl	when	talks about the best hotels?
The carpenter is a craftsman	why	loves his job.
To		do you wish to speak?
Wimbledon is a club	whom	is usually quiet and peaceful.

____

____

____

____

____

____

____

____

____

____

2 Look at the following expressions from Unit 7. Write each expression in the comparative and superlative forms.

Example: *fundamental skill / a more fundamental skill / the most fundamental skill*

a early stages ____________________

____

b reasonable standard ____________________

____

c good spelling skills ____________________

____

d decent CV ____________________

____

e bad spelling ____________________

____

f recent years ____________________

____

3 Select expressions from Activity B2 to complete the following sentences.

a Of all the applicants, the ______________ was George's, which is why he got the job.

b I think students' ______________ has got worse because they do not read books.

c The ______________ of a child's development are very important.

d I think we should ask for a ______________ from our applicants.

e There has been a huge increase in the consumption of sugar levels in ______________.

f Full marks were awarded to essays with the ______________.

4 Make compound nouns using the words in the box.

Example: *side* + *walk* = *sidewalk*

board	break	bus	cooked	cut	fast
full	hair	machine	moon	over (x2)	
pool	ripe	rise	~~side~~	soft	spotting
stop	sun	swimming	train	under (x2)	
~~walk~~	ware	washing	weight	white	world

____

____

____

____

____

5 Choose five compound nouns from Activity B4 and use them in your own sentences.

Example: *In British English, the* ***sidewalk*** *is called the pavement.*

____

____

____

____

____

C Skills

1 There is a programme on television called *Dirty Jobs*.

a What do you think the programme is about?

____

b List **three** dirty jobs that you would not like to do.

____

____

____

2 Skim the text *Dirty Jobs* and find words that have similar meanings to the words and phrases below.

- **a** presenter (paragraph 1) ____________________
- **b** a result of (4) ____________________
- **c** jobs (1) ____________________
- **d** very visual (4) ____________________
- **e** with (1) ____________________
- **f** received large numbers of (4) ____________________
- **g** test (1) ____________________
- **h** paid for (4) ____________________
- **i** combination (2) ____________________
- **j** idea (4) ____________________
- **k** humour (2) ____________________
- **l** credit (4) ____________________
- **m** dangers (3) ____________________

Dirty Jobs

[1] *Dirty Jobs* is a programme on the Discovery Channel in which the host, Mike Rowe, is shown performing difficult, strange and/or messy occupational duties alongside the typical employees. The show started with three pilot episodes in November 2003, and continued until 12th September 2012 with a total of 169 episodes.

[2] The appeal of the show is the juxtaposition of Mike Rowe, a well-spoken man of television with a sharp, sarcastic wit, the situations in which he's put and the colourful personalities of the men and women who actually do that job for a living.

[3] A worker takes on Rowe as a fully involved assistant during a typical day at work, during which he works hard to complete every task as best he can despite discomfort, hazards or situations that are just plain disgusting. The 'dirty job' often includes the cameraman and rest of the crew getting just as dirty as Rowe.

[4] The show is a spin-off from a local San Francisco programme called *Somebody's Gotta Do It* that host Mike Rowe once did. After completing a graphic piece on cows and dairy farming, Rowe was inundated with letters expressing 'shock, horror, fascination, disbelief and wonder'. Rowe then sent the tape to the Discovery Channel, which commissioned a series based on this concept. Mike stated that he originally wanted to honour his father, a lifetime pig farmer, by bringing fame to the less-than-glorious careers.

Adapted from http://en.wikipedia.org

3 Read the text in more detail, then complete the notes below.

Programme name **(a)** ______________ on **(b)** ______________ Channel. Show started in **(c)** ______________ with **(d)** ______________ episodes and ended in **(e)** ______________. Three things that are appealing about the show: the presenter, **(f)** ______________ and **(g)** the ______________.

Those getting dirty include Rowe, **(h)** ______________ and **(i)** ______________. Rowe works alongside other workers doing things that are uncomfortable, **(j)** ______________ or **(k)** ______________.

Originally, show called **(l)** ______________.

4 **Here are some of the dirty jobs that were shown in the series. Match the job to the description and then rank them according to how much you would like to do each one. Put the job you would least like to do at the top of your list.**

alligator farmer	A person who works underground to extract valuable minerals.
plumber	Someone who removes from the roads animals killed by traffic.
coal miner	Somebody who has to climb up skyscrapers to keep them clean.
roadkill cleaner	A person who keeps the underground tunnels of the city clean from waste.
high-rise window washer	Residential and commercial rubbish is collected and separated by this person.
leather tanner	This person gives total care and protection to this reptile.
sewer inspector	Someone who cleans and treats animal hides for general use.
rubbish collector	Someone who deals with all aspects of water systems in buildings.

5 **Look at the advert below for the job of airport baggage handler. List three things that you think a baggage handler has to do and three things that you think make it a 'dirty job'.**

WANTED

Part-time airport baggage handlers (three needed)

Location: Airport Terminal 1
Salary: \$10–\$17 per hour, depending on shift hours, experience and age
Start date: 31st May
Job type: Part-time, temporary
Hours: 10–15 hours per week, including weekends and nights (suitable for students)
Requirements: Applicants need to be fit and healthy, as the position involves lifting and carrying. No formal academic qualifications are required, although preference is given to applicants with IGCSE English and Maths.

Note: As the job involves working outside in all weathers, a uniform is provided.

We are now recruiting baggage handlers for Terminal 1. This is a part-time, temporary position and shifts will range from 10–15 hours per week, depending on flight schedules. There are overtime opportunities when flight schedules increase. The job duties will include loading and offloading baggage to/from aircraft, and moving baggage to airport carousels for passengers to collect.

To apply, send an email with relevant information to: vacancies@airportterminal1.com

Baggage handler tasks	What makes it a dirty job?

6 **Which type of person is the job of airport baggage handler good for? Mark each one with a tick or a cross.**

a Someone who likes working outside. ☐

b Someone who likes being with people. ☐

c Someone who likes to wear their own clothes. ☐

d Someone with no qualifications. ☐

e Someone who is physically strong. ☐

f Someone who is not available at weekends. ☐

g Someone who can work at night. ☐

h Someone who wants a full-time position. ☐

i Someone who is happy with a temporary position. ☐

Writing

7 **You are going to apply for the job of airport baggage handler. Write your email and include all the relevant information you need for the application.**

Unit 8: Focus on listening skills

A Vocabulary

1 In the wordsearch, there are **12** words that you might find in a CV. Find the words, then put each one into the correct category. There are two words for each category.

R	A	G	S	K	W	V	M	I	F	L	U	E	N	T
C	F	R	E	U	A	M	O	L	P	I	D	T	R	U
Y	Q	L	C	N	H	V	E	H	G	O	Z	W	H	A
R	N	V	O	T	D	S	R	O	A	Y	F	B	D	T
A	S	R	N	G	O	E	O	U	G	I	K	D	J	I
T	R	G	D	Y	M	X	R	R	S	D	R	A	O	K
N	J	O	A	N	S	I	L	L	S	E	O	J	L	A
E	P	P	R	I	M	A	R	Y	S	C	H	O	O	L
M	A	A	Y	H	Q	I	N	S	Z	R	B	C	A	E
E	R	Y	S	S	H	E	R	A	I	F	L	K	B	V
L	T	G	C	B	A	S	K	E	T	B	A	L	L	E
E	T	K	H	C	U	L	E	M	X	D	R	L	S	L
P	I	G	O	O	R	A	X	L	D	T	J	A	R	S
D	M	W	O	L	W	Y	C	V	B	Y	V	W	I	D
L	E	B	L	W	D	R	G	N	I	D	A	E	R	N

Places	Hobbies	Languages	Qualifications	Personal information	Work experience

2 In Unit 8, you saw the words *employer* and *employee*. *Employer* is the doer and *employee* is the recipient. In the table below are some similar words. Fill in the gaps in the table.

Giver	Recipient
Interviewer	
	Trainee
Payer	
Nominator	
	Advisee

3 Use the correct form of the word from Activity A2 to complete the following sentences.

a There are 20 ______________ in the class and only 15 desks for them!

b The ______________ sat nervously, waiting to be called in.

c On a cheque, you clearly write the name of the ______________ on the top line.

d The ______________ had a good look at all the CVs before inviting everyone for an interview.

e You are not the only ______________ for the award, as there are 12 others.

4 Which words can you relate to each of the categories below? Add **at least four** words to each spidergram. All the words are in Unit 8.

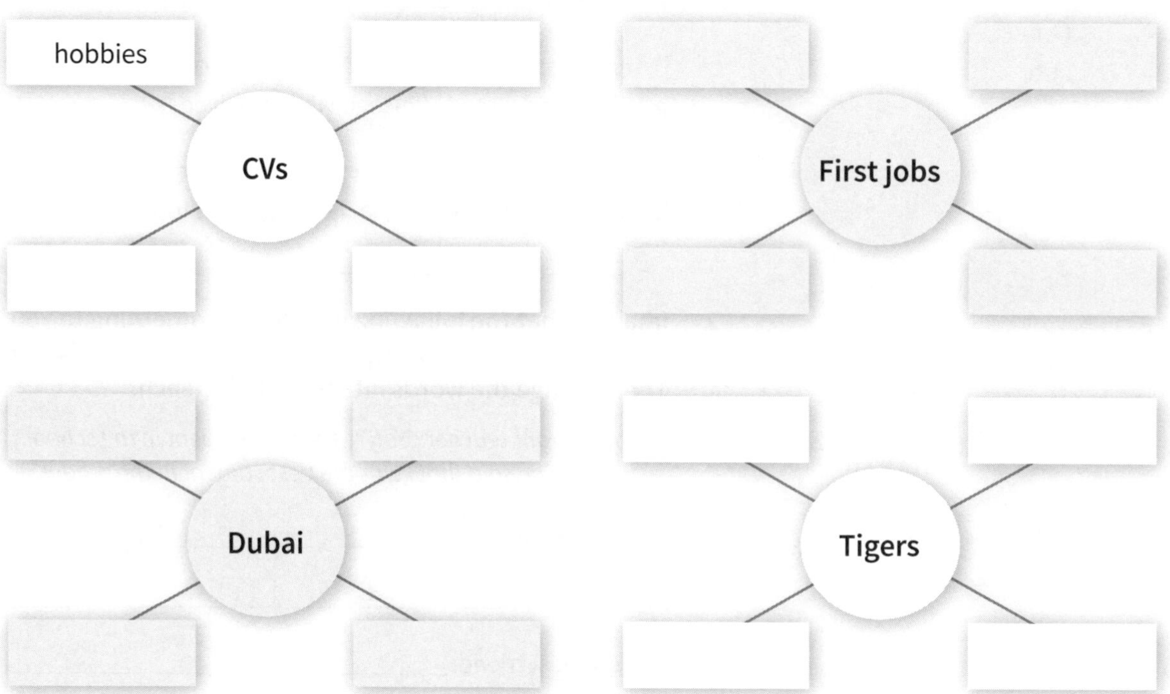

B Use of English

1 **Look at these sentences from Unit 8:**

'So what information would you say is essential?'

'That's an interesting idea – I like that!'

In reported speech, tenses, word order and pronouns may change:

Pablo asked what information was essential.

Pablo said that was an interesting idea and that he liked it.

Change the following into reported speech. You can decide who is speaking (for example Pablo, he, she).

a 'We're meeting them outside the coffee shop.'

____

b 'Be quiet. The children are sleeping.'

____

c 'I'll make sure that everybody gets a turn.'

____

d 'We lived in America for six years.'

____

e 'I was walking home when I saw the accident.'

____

f 'They've always been very generous with me.'

____

g 'They had already finished when I arrived.'

____

h 'I didn't go to the cinema, because I was too tired.'

____

2 Imagine that the following people say something to you. Write what you think they would say, or what you would like them to say to you. Then change the words into reported speech.

Example: *Your teacher: 'You're the best student in the school.'*
She said that I was the best student in the school.

a Your teacher: ______________________________

____

b Your best friend: ______________________________

____

c Your favourite sports personality: ______________________________

____

d An adult in your family: ______________________________

____

e Someone you admire: ______________________________

____

3 Sibylle has just been talking to her teacher and now she is telling her friend what her teacher said. Underline the reporting phrases.

Example: *She claimed that I was a good student, but that I could do better.*

a She told me I should try to get into university.

b She advised me to think about what courses I would like to do.

c She ordered me to study every night.

d She asked me if my parents wanted me to go to university.

e She enquired if I could afford to go to university.

f She observed that I only had one brother.

g She announced that she would do anything to help me.

4 **Complete the following sentences using one of the reporting phrases from Activity B3. You may find you can use more than one.**

a She ________________________ the way to the bus station.

b She ________________________ that they were getting married.

c She ________________________ to tidy my bedroom.

d She ________________ that I had been arriving late to my lessons.

e She proudly ________________________ that she had written the assignment by herself.

f She ________________________ to go to the doctor immediately.

g She ________________________ to leave my work on her desk.

h She ______________ if I had thought about doing something different.

C Skills

1 **In Unit 8 of the Coursebook, Sophie Labane wrote a CV. Look at the job advertisements opposite and decide which would be the best job for Sophie. Give four reasons for your first choice and four reasons why you did not choose the other two jobs.**

Casual office worker needed

We're looking for a young person, who loves an office environment, to help with casual work at the weekends. The candidate should have some office experience and some higher-education qualifications. We are a French international company, so French is a prerequisite.

Babysitter required

Want to earn some money looking after young children by babysitting? We're a young, busy couple setting up our own business and need somebody to look after our children at the weekends. You'll be required to cook and clean up after the children and remain in the home while we're at work.

Youth group leader

We need a fun person to contribute to our youth group. Do you:

- like mixing with people who have the same interests?
- enjoy the outdoors?
- speak English?
- enjoy sport?

Job choice: ________________________

Reasons: ________________________

____

____

____

____

____

____

____

Writing

2 Sophie has written an application for the job, but the information is not in the right order. Rewrite her application.

- Since I am still at school, I tend to be free at the weekends and evenings.
- I enjoy sport and mixing with people who have the same interests. For this reason, I am a member of a fan club of my favourite basketball team.
- I am fluent in both Swahili and English, which I believe is a requirement, although Swahili is my first language.
- I enjoy being outdoors, as I like to watch basketball teams playing and practising.
- Dear Sir/Madam,
- Sophie Labane
- I hope this application is viewed positively and I look forward to hearing from you soon. I have attached my contact details and CV with this letter.
- Yours faithfully,
- I recently saw your advertisement for a _______________ and I would be interested in applying for this position. I think I would be a strong candidate for the following reasons:

____

____

____

____

____

____

____

____

____

____

____

Unit 9: Focus on reading skills

A Vocabulary

1 Look at the numbers below. Write them as a list of figures in the correct numerical order.

- **a** one hundred and eighty-three
- **b** one thousand, two hundred and thirty-six
- **c** eleven hundred and thirty-seven
- **d** one hundred and thirty-five thousand, two hundred and eighty-four
- **e** one hundred and fifty-three thousand, two hundred and eighty-four
- **f** one hundred and thirty-five thousand, two hundred and forty-eight
- **g** eighty-three thousand and one
- **h** six hundred and thirty-one million, two hundred and fifty-six thousand, seven hundred and twenty-one
- **i** twenty-three

- **a** 23
- **b** ______________
- **c** ______________
- **d** ______________
- **e** ______________
- **f** ______________
- **g** ______________
- **h** ______________
- **i** ______________

2 Use the numbers in the box to complete the information opposite.

1/3	15,141.65 litres	314,000%	
13	680 kilograms	10 centimetres	
50,000	1000	7 billion	a week
492 seconds	1 million		

- **a** Jumbo jets use ______________ of fuel to take off.
- **b** It takes six months to build a Rolls Royce and ______________ hours to build a Toyota.
- **c** The average person eats almost ______________ of food a year.
- **d** It takes ______________ for sunlight to reach the earth.
- **e** There are ______________ ants for every person in the world.
- **f** Earth experiences ______________ earthquakes each year.
- **g** The annual growth of internet traffic is ______________.
- **h** There are more than ______________ chemicals in a cup of coffee.
- **i** ______________ of all cancers are sun-related.
- **j** The world population reached ______________ in 2012.
- **k** Over the last 150 years, the average height of people in industrialised nations has increased by ______________.
- **l** A person can live without food for about a month, but only for about ______________ without water.

3 Complete the crossword.

Clues

Across

3 To die or cease to exist (6)

6 The action of cutting off a person's arm or leg (10)

7 A person who travels in search of information (8)

9 Try to stop someone from doing something (8)

10 A fixed amount of food or water (7)

Down

1 A place where food and other things are stored (5)

2 A severe snowstorm (8)

4 Acting wildly or violently (6)

5 Walked unsteadily and almost fell (8)

8 Written clearly enough to be read (7)

4 Reorder the words below to make sentences.

Example: *men the hundreds were of tragedy injured in*

Hundreds of men were injured in the tragedy.

a and the debut a was huge actor's out success a sell

____

b misleading the he were so mistakes instructions many made

____

c but they resembled other they twins not each identical were

____

d to house the directions gave get about how he to precise

____

e because so was hair she her braided it long

____

f which the on house was the government land built to the local belonged

____

g brave soldier it was for a to thing do a

____

h valued the weapon and was a traditional saber very

____

B Use of English

1 Look at these sentences from the text on page 54. What tenses are the underlined verbs?

a Josef (i) <u>has refused</u> to give up work. At the age of 98, the head of one of the world's best-known folk-dance groups (ii) <u>continues</u> to go to work every day and (iii) <u>takes part</u> in training dancers.

b A small, dapper figure, Josef (iv) <u>has kept</u> the distinguished and stylish looks that (v) <u>helped</u> him in his first career as a classical dancer at one of the world's greatest dance theatres.

(i) ______________________________

(ii) ______________________________

(iii) ______________________________

(iv) ______________________________

(v) ______________________________

2 **When we write about living people, we often need to use the three tenses from Activity B1. Which of the tenses do we use for the following?**

a finished events in the past ______________

b life experiences ______________

c current habits ______________

3 **Underline one example of each tense in the following paragraph. Say why the tense has been used.**

> Last month, I finally achieved an Olympic medal in race walking after many years of hard work. I have tried for years to get to the top of my sport and there were so many barriers along the way, but finally I got there. Unfortunately, people don't take the sport very seriously because it doesn't have the excitement that sports such as the 100 metres sprint or high-jump have. It's not an attractive sport and people often laugh and make fun of the way you walk because it looks unnatural. Training can also be quite lonely, particularly when the weather is cold and wet. But despite all the odds, I did it – I achieved my dream and now everybody wants to know me!

Example: *achieved = past simple tense, because the action of 'achieving' happened last month*

____

____

4 **Complete the information about two athletes, using the correct tense of the verb in brackets.**

Mohamed 'Mo' Farah ______________ (*to be*) a Somali-born British track and field athlete. He ______________ (*win*) the Olympic and World Championship medals in the 10,000 and 5000 metres running. He ______________ (*to be born*) in 1983 in Somalia and ______________ (*move*) to Britain to join his father, without knowing any English, when he ______________ (*to be*) eight. He ______________ (*to be*) a fan of Arsenal football club and ______________ (*train*) with the team's players.

Usain Bolt ______________ (*to be*) a Jamaican sprinter and widely ______________ (*regard*) as the fastest person ever. Also known as 'Lightning Bolt', he ______________ (*hold*) the 100 and 200 metre world records. He ______________ (*born*) in 1986 and, as a child, he ______________ (*play*) cricket and football with his brother in the street. He ______________ (*become*) a professional athlete in 2004. His autobiography ______________ (*release*) recently and in it he ______________ (*comment*) that 'life should be exciting, it's my life and I ______________ (*to be*) a cool and exciting guy.'

5 Write a short paragraph about somebody you admire. Make sure you use all three tenses.

____

____

____

____

____

____

____

C Skills

1 Look at this title for an article you are going to read. What do you think the article is about?

Folk maestro looks back on life in dance

a A person who knows about different types of dance. ☐

b A famous traditional dancer who is now too old to dance. ☐

c A young dancer talking about another famous dancer. ☐

2 Skim the text below and find these numbers. What do they refer to?

Example: *98= age the ex-dancer is at the time of the interview*

a 12 ______________________

b 1955 ______________________

c 1906 ______________________

d 1943 ______________________

e 1920 ______________________

f Fifty ______________________

g 1937 ______________________

h 1945 ______________________

Folk maestro looks back on life in dance

A world-famous dancer has refused to give up work even though he is 98 years old. He is the head of one of the world's best-known folk-dance groups and continues to go to work every day and takes part in training dancers.

A small, dapper figure, Josef has kept the distinguished and stylish looks that helped him in his first career as a classical dancer at one of the world's greatest dance theatres.

'I think I'm the only one, not just in dance, but in any area, who works at the age of 98,' says Josef. 'I don't want to retire.' The Artistic Director of both the group and its training school spends several hours each day at work, aided by his younger wife, who, like the other staff, is one of his former dancers.

'Josef enjoys going to the young children's lessons most of all because they inspire him and give him hope for the future,' says the Director of the school, which trains dancers from the age of 12 for a possible place in the group.

Born in 1906, Josef first got interested in dance while travelling across the countryside with his aunts, who worked as teachers. In 1920, his father enrolled him in a dance school, hoping that dance would give him the skills that a young man needs. He then moved quickly up the career ladder, but his dream was to perform folk dance professionally and, in 1937, he formed a small company. In 1945, the company became the first dance group to travel abroad and, in 1955, toured many countries in Europe, where Josef recalled that the group was particularly enthusiastic about watching 'Scottish dancers in kilts'.

Like many cultural organisations, the dance group receives finance from the government and it is just as popular today as it was in the past. But, increasingly, there are some differences, and one that is becoming an international phenomenon, namely that pop music is beginning to overshadow the folk heritage.

Nonetheless, the dance company's tradition is set to continue as long as the group's school, which was founded in 1943, keeps training new generations of dancers. Fifty pupils of both sexes graduate every four years, with the best joining the dance group.

Adapted from www.moscowtimes.ru

3 Write a sentence for each of the numbers.

Example: *At the age of 98, Josef still goes into work every day.*

a 12 ______________________________

b 1955 ______________________________

c 1906 ______________________________

d 1943 ______________________________

e 1920 ______________________________

f Fifty ______________________________

g 1937 ______________________________

h 1945 ______________________________

4 Identify the errors in the sentences below, then rewrite each sentence so that the information is correct.

Example: *Josef no longer goes to work every day.*
Josef continues to go to work every day.

a He first became a folk dancer at one of the world's greatest dance theatres.

____

b His wife used to be his manager.

____

c All his dancers are guaranteed a place in his dance group.

____

d His mother thought that dance would be important.

____

e Josef was mainly interested in pop music.

____

f He travelled to America in 1945.

____

g The government occasionally gives support to his group.

____

h He does not think that folk dance is as popular as pop music.

____

i Every year, pupils graduate from the school.

____

Writing

5 **Choose one of the people illustrated on the left and write a short piece about them, like the article on page 54. Write 150–200 words (Extended) or 100–150 words (Core).**

Imagine what the person has achieved and try to include information about:

- their name, nationality, date and place of birth
- their family background
- how they became interested in their activity
- how they achieved their ambitions
- their future ambitions and how they intend to achieve them
- how their ambitions have affected their personal lives
- what drives them in their ambitions.

Unit 10: Focus on reading and writing skills

A Vocabulary

1 **There are 16 adjectives in the word circle below. Each adjective describes a person's character. Circle the adjectives.**

well-organisedpeacefulbalancedambitioussociablethoughtfulsensitivepassivereliableopen-mindedaggressiveimaginativebenevolentdominantactiveoptimistic

2 **Write an adjective from Activity A1 next to its synonym.**

a desiring success ______________

b busy ______________

c believing positively ______________

d superior, controlling ______________

e kind ______________

f creative ______________

g combative ______________

h receptive ______________

i trustworthy ______________

j non-violent ______________

k responsive ______________

l caring, mindful ______________

m friendly ______________

n efficient ______________

o serene ______________

p equalised ______________

3 **What do you think are the qualities and characteristics of a) a politician and b) a yoga teacher? Separate the adjectives from Activity A1 into two categories. Give each person eight adjectives, but be careful – some adjectives could apply to both.**

Politician	Yoga teacher

4 **How would you describe yourself? Write down four adjectives.**

a ______________________________

b ______________________________

c ______________________________

d ______________________________

5 Fill in the gaps to complete the 'signpost' words and phrases.

a a_ _ _

b b_ _ _ _ _ _

c b_ _

d c_ _ _ _ _ _ _ _ _ _ _

e h_ _ _ _ _ _

f i_/s_ _ _ _/o_

g o_/t_ _/o_ _ _ _/h_ _ _

h o_ _ _ _ _ _ _ _

i t_ _ _ _ _ _ _ _

j u_ _ _ _ _

6 Use signpost words and phrases to complete the text below, written by a student about homework.

For many students, having to do homework is the worst thing about school life. Some students complain about homework **(a)** ______________ it takes away their free time. **(b)** ______________ , despite their protests, most students just get on and do whatever homework they have been given. **(c)** ______________ , it is often rushed and not done particularly well; of course, there are other students who do not do their homework at all **(d)** ______________ someone forces them to.

Teachers usually set homework for a very good reason: to give students an opportunity to practise things learnt in class and to develop various skills. **(e)** ______________ some students do not realise this and **(f)** ______________ consider homework as a waste of time. Students need to understand that homework is an important part of learning, and we need to do it, **(g)** ______________ we will suffer in the long run. I've heard some students complaining that homework stops them from doing any physical exercise, **(h)** ______________ of course this is nonsense! It is just a poor excuse, **(i)** ______________ nowadays we get plenty of opportunities for physical activity at school.

(j) ______________ understanding how important homework is, I **(k)** ______________ don't particularly like it. **(l)** ______________ , I recognise that teachers give us homework for our benefit, and not for theirs.

7 Underline the signpost words in the phrases in the list below, then draw a line to match the phrases to make complete sentences.

a Computer games are getting cheaper.	**i)** therefore, unable to play.
b In order to complete the task,	**ii)** a great day was had by all.
c So to summarise,	**iii)** In other words, I don't think he'll be home early.
d They are a strong group.	**iv)** However, they are not as strong as the last one.
e We have got many different colours,	**v)** for example grey, yellow and red.
f He was injured and,	**vi)** most importantly, they are not allowed sweets.
g They can eat fruit every day, but	**vii)** you have to follow the instructions carefully.
h Girls have to wear skirts and,	**viii)** more specifically, grey ones.
i He has a meeting this evening.	**ix)** Furthermore, their quality is also improving.
j They didn't attend the seminars and	**x)** for this reason they were not promoted.

B Use of English

1 Complete the sentences on page 59, using a preposition from the box below.

for (x 2)	to (x 3)	from	in	on

a He apologised ______________ being late again.

b He was made to apologise ______________ the headteacher for being late again.

c She spent many days caring ______________ her sick daughter.

d Has her daughter recovered ______________ her illness yet?

e You have to work harder if you want to succeed ______________ your examinations.

f Her essay is based ______________ a real-life experience she had.

g It is very annoying when people do not respond ______________ emails.

h They all agreed ______________ arrive early.

2 Write complete sentences using the correct noun + preposition from the middle two columns of the table below.

Example: *There was a lot of damage to property due to the flooding.*

~~There was a lot of~~	hold	with	~~property due to the flooding.~~
a People should	control	to	emails when they receive them.
b There has been an increase in the	cure	~~to~~	honey throughout the country.
c All children are immunised now a	ban	for	polio has been found.
d They had another	grudge	over	their neighbours about the dog.
e They will be	quarrel	for	the headteachers later today.
f The boys have finally got a good	grasp	on	how to play the game.
g There should always be parental	demand	on	how much the Internet is used.
h He could not	~~damage~~	against	any longer and fell.
i They are trying to bring in a	meeting	of	smoking in the car with children in it.
j They always argue as they have a	reply	with	each other.

a ______________________________

b ______________________________

c ______________________________

d ______________________________

e ______________________________

f ______________________________

g ______________________________

h ______________________________

i ______________________________

j ______________________________

C Skills

1 Look at the pictures below. Who is this? What did he achieve?

____

____

____

____

2 Complete the sentence below using the words in the box.

skydiver sound barrier capsule space helium balloon Austrian dangerous extreme

Felix Baumgartner is an **(a)** ______________ daredevil and **(b)** ______________ , who broke the **(c)** ______________ with an extremely **(d)** ______________ jump from **(e)** ______________ . He first travelled to **(f)** ______________ heights in a **(g)** ______________ , which was towed by a huge **(h)** ______________ kilometres above Earth – and then he made the jump.

3 Look again at the adjectives in Activity A1. Which would you use to describe Felix Baumgartner?

____

____

4 You are going to read about Felix Baumgartner. Before you read, look at the words and phrases from the text in the left-hand column and draw a line to match them to their meaning.

a sound barrier	**i)** The occurrence of two or more unplanned things at the same time.
b helium	**ii)** Crying.
c capsule	**iii)** A reckless and very daring person.
d daredevil	**iv)** Pulled.
e towed	**v)** An act or achievement that shows courage, strength or skill.
f freefall	**vi)** To send something into outer space or the air.
g launch	**vii)** A sudden increase in air resistance to something nearing the speed of sound.
h weeping	**viii)** A gas that is lighter than air.
i famed	**ix)** A small part of a spacecraft.
j incidents	**x)** A fast or continuing drop.
k coincidentally	**xi)** Famous, well known.
l feat	**xii)** Events or occurrences.

5 Look at these seven phrases. Which ones do you think you will read in the text? Give reasons.

a Swiss nationality.

b Four times the speed of a cruise liner.

c During the fall, he travelled at an average speed of 1357.64 kilometres per hour.

d He broke the current freefall record.

e Everything looks green.

f It was the first time his parents had travelled outside of Europe.

____

____

____

____

____

____

____

____

____

6 Skim the text and check your answers to Activities C4 and C5.

Felix Baumgartner broke the world's freefall record by jumping 39 kilometres above the earth and breaking the sound barrier.

Felix Baumgartner, an Austrian 43-year-old former military parachutist, floated for two hours in a purpose-built capsule towed by an enormous helium balloon before leaping into the record books from a height equivalent to almost four times the height of a cruising passenger airline. During the fall, he travelled at an average speed of 1357.64 kilometres per hour.

He broke the current freefall record of 31.3 kilometres held by Joe Kittinger. Mr Kittinger, who set his record in 1960, was the only person allowed to communicate with Mr Baumgartner while he was inside the capsule which carried him into space.

As the launch began, Mr Kittinger told Mr Baumgartner: 'You're doing great, Felix. Doing great. Everything looks green and you are on your way to space.'

Mr Baumgartner's parents were in Roswell, New Mexico for the launch, the first time they had travelled outside of Europe. His mother could be seen weeping as her daredevil son launched into space.

While the action took place in the city of Roswell, famed for space-related incidents, attention was worldwide, with millions watching it online.

Coincidentally, Baumgartner's attempted feat also marked the 65th anniversary of US test pilot Chuck Yeager's successful attempt to become the first man to officially break the sound barrier aboard an aeroplane.

As well as becoming the first man to break the sound barrier unaided, Baumgartner set three other world records during the attempt.

The first came after two hours and two minutes when he broke the record for the highest manned balloon flight, breaking the record of Malcolm Ross and Victor Prather, who soared to 34.668 metres in 1961. Their record ended in tragedy when Prather drowned in the Gulf of Mexico upon landing.

Adapted from www.telegraph.co.uk/science

7 Read the text again and answer these questions.

a What was Felix's job before he completed this feat?

____

b What two references does the word *leaping* have in the text?

____

c What comparison is given about the height he jumped from?

____

d Who was he in contact with and why was that person also famous?

____

e What had also happened on this day 65 years ago?

____

f What was the first achievement of Felix's feat?

____

g How had others faired in this attempt?

____

h In what way was the colour green significant?

____

Writing

8 You have decided to tell your school youth club about Felix Baumgartner. First, you need to make some notes in order to prepare your talk. Which three of the following headings do you think would be suitable to help you make your notes? Why?

- Home and education
- Nationality
- Physical skills
- Family
- Character
- Achievements

Make **three** notes under each heading.

Example: *Home and education*

• *Born in Salzburg, Austria.*

____

____

____

____

____

____

____

____

____

____

____

____

____

____

____

____

____

____

____

Unit 11: Focus on writing skills

A Vocabulary

1 The words in the box can all be found in Unit 11 of your Coursebook. Find them in the word spiral and circle them. One has been done as an example.

peer	compromised	preferential
counterparts	prevalent	curricula
sanitary	discriminate	~~self-esteem~~
neglects	transition	vulnerable
nutritional	adequate	

```
                                    S X
H N E G L E C T S G B H U Q C J W   E T
Z C F A C I M R S V A X L F U Q H   L H
V O                           R Q   F S
X U   X G E M D I N E V U P   Y D   - A
C N   O T C U R R I C U L A   X I   E N
O T   N R                 N D   D S   S I
M E   Q A   N S E O B   H E   E C   T T
P R   D N   K P I X Y   Z Q   E R   E A
R P   Y S   P R   X D   Y U   O I   E R
O A   V I   P T   N D   N A   Y M   M Y
M R   U T   E H         O T   Q I   N F
I T   T I   E W X B L T O E   W N   L J
S S   Z O   R V S V H R J N   N A   O P
E V   C N                     F T   U O
D L   O E G L V U L N E R A B L E   T M
P R   X Z N U T R I T I O N A L G   C L
A F                                 L F
X Z D G P R E F E R E N T I A L J S E N
B X X A V K V N P R E V A L E N T A Q X
```

2 Use the words from Activity A1 to complete the sentences.

a There is little ______________ value in a stick of celery.

b He has very low ______________ and this affects his classwork and number of friends.

c There are ______________ books for all students to receive one copy each.

d No child should be given ______________ treatment; they should all be treated equally.

e There is a lot of ______________ pressure at school, forcing children to do things they do not want to do.

f The ______________ from childhood to adulthood can sometimes be very difficult.

g The conditions at the camp were not ______________, resulting in illnesses.

h His ______________ at work have become very uncooperative towards him.

i Animals can be very ______________, which is why we should not hurt them.

j They had a big argument, but then they ______________ and everything is fine now.

k This is ______________ amongst many people in this part of the world.

l The ______________ at the schools have not changed and are not suited to modern learning.

m At school, you are taught to ______________ between good and bad literature.

n He ______________ the lessons that he is not interested in and this affects his overall grade.

3 **Put each of the words in the box below into an appropriate category in the table. Choose three words for each category, but be warned – some may fit into more than one category!**

winds tradition
shells shade lens
atmosphere literature
diving wild hunt
dictionary rope
danger whale
heat museum
species catamaran
heights water
spelling waves
theatre camera

	1	2	3
Marine life	diving	shells	whale
Language learning			
Animal life			
Mountain climbing			
Photography			
Desert adventure			
Sailing			
History/culture			

4 **Use the words in the table to write a meaningful and grammatically correct sentence.**

Example: *While I was out diving for shells in deep waters, I saw a whale!*

a ______________________________

b ______________________________

c ______________________________

d ______________________________

e ______________________________

f ______________________________

g ______________________________

B Use of English

1 **Look at the following sentences with *either/or*, *neither/nor* and decide if they are correct or not. Rewrite the incorrect sentences.**

a Neither Sara nor Emily do as they are told.

____

b Either the teacher or the secretary has the keys to the classroom.

____

c Either the dogs or the cat has to go.

____

d Hassan could not find the key neither on nor under the mat.

____

e She did not find her purse either on or under the sofa.

____

f He neither mentioned the test nor his result.

____

2 Match the explanations i–vi below to the sentences a–e in Activity B1.

i) This is incorrect because it is a double negative. ______________

ii) This is correct – both subjects are singular, so the helping verb *have* is singular. ______________

iii) This is incorrect – both subjects are singular, so the helping verb *do* should also be singular and in the third person. ______________

iv) If one of the subjects is plural then the verb also has to be plural, so this is incorrect. ______________

v) Both *either* and *or* are used correctly here. ______________

vi) Both *neither* and *nor* are used correctly here. ______________

3 Complete the paragraph below using the adjectives in the box.

broadest   blue   stunning   sandy   small   steep   wide

Positioned right at the top of the Caribbean island chain, this group of 36 **(a)** ______________ islands is characterised by **(b)** ______________ green hills and white **(c)** ______________ beaches. Around them lie the clear **(d)** ______________ waters of the Sir Francis Drake Channel. This **(e)** ______________ environment is perfect for a **(f)** ______________ range of water sports – that's why we offer our **(g)** ______________ variety of adventure training programmes here.

4 Here is a definition of an adjective, but the words are mixed up. Rewrite it correctly.

make describes an interesting adjective a more noun pronoun or to it.

____

5 If you use more than one adjective for a description, the adjectives must follow a particular order. However, it is rare to use more than three adjectives together. Write two or three adjectives for each category in the table below. Some examples have been done for you.

Feeling	Size	Age	Shape	Colour	Origin	Material
idyllic			rectangular			sandy

6 Complete the following sentences, using the adjectives in brackets. Remember to put them in the correct order and in the correct position in the sentence.

Example: *I really like that car that is always parked opposite. (old, big, black)*

I really like that big, old, black car that is always parked opposite.

a My brother has a horse. (*young, white, beautiful*)

____

b George was given a clock for his birthday. (*antique, gold, Italian*)

____

c There was a box on the shelf. (*red, square, wooden*)

____

d She put an ornament on her desk. (*plastic, disgusting, fluorescent*)

____

e Maria has just bought some sunglasses. (*French, new, trendy*)

____

f He was wearing a pair of gloves. (*leather, lovely, new*)

____

7 Write two adjectives that could be used to describe the following.

a a tree ______________________________

b a meal ______________________________

c your favourite place ______________________________

d an ugly object that you do not like

____

C Skills

1 You are going to read a text called *It's the coldest, most isolated continent on Earth. Why would anyone want to work there?* What job and place do you think the passage is about?

____

2 Look at the following words and phrases. Do you think they will appear in the text? Why, or why not?

Example: *Arctic – No, because it is not the most isolated continent in the world*

a Antarctic

____

b densely populated

____

c high salary

____

d northern hemisphere

____

e penguins

____

f tropical

____

g polar bears

____

3 The words and phrases below have been removed from the text. Use paper or digital reference sources to help you find out what they mean.

a auroral ______________________________

b motives ______________________________

c devoted ______________________________

d applicants ______________________________

e reigns ______________________________

f insomnia ______________________________

g swell ______________________________

h founded ______________________________

i maintain ______________________________

j tang ______________________________

4 Write the words in Activity C3 next to the correct synonyms below.

a light ______________________

b established ______________________

c continues ______________________

d flavour ______________________

e increase ______________________

f look after ______________________

g reasons to do something ______________________

h sleeplessness ______________________

i candidates ______________________

j committed ______________________

5 Read the text and fill in the gaps with the words from Activity C3.

It's the coldest, most isolated continent on Earth. Why would anyone want to work there?

Applications are pouring in from chefs to studentships in response to an advert placed by the British Antarctic Survey (BAS) to work in Antarctica. The BAS is looking for people to **(a)** ______________ its southernmost research centre, the Halley base, during the continent's four-month summer.

Antarctica is the coldest and windiest continent on Earth, and significant dates that **(b)** ______________ would look forward to are sun-down (last day the sun can be seen) on 29th April and sun-up (first day when the sun rises after winter) on 13th August. The Halley base was originally **(c)** ______________ in 1956; Halley VI was officially opened in February 2013 and is dedicated to the study of the earth's atmosphere. Each year, 15 staff see out the long winter, when temperatures fall as low as –55˚C and darkness **(d)** ______________ for 105 days, relieved only by the spectacular **(e)** ______________ displays.

Even in summer, when numbers on the base **(f)** ______________ to 65, temperatures can plummet to –28˚C. Many staff develop chronic polar **(g)** ______________ because of the 24-hour daylight.

Everybody longs for fresh fruit and vegetables, since food supplies arrive just twice a year and must be dragged 12 kilometres from the coast. One former staff member recalls his colleagues fantasising endlessly about the **(h)** ______________ of tomatoes.

Applicants for the jobs need to be sure that they can get on with the team, as the nearest neighbours are 30 kilometres away and rather short on conversation, being emperor penguins. The centre is best known for its work in monitoring the hole in the ozone layer, but it also studies atmospheric pollution, sea-level rise, climate change and geology.

But while scientists have often **(i)** ______________ their lives to examining particular phenomena, support staff on the base have other **(j)** ______________. Many find that working in the Antarctic is an ideal way to save money: pay for a studentship is £13,863 a year; all accommodation, food and clothing come free; and there is nowhere to spend any money.

Adapted from an article by Tania Branigan in *The Guardian*.

6 Answer the following questions.

a What is the weather like in Antarctica? Give **two** pieces of information.

____

b What is the difference between the lowest summer and winter temperatures?

____

c What happens to many people because of the 24-hour daylight in summer?

____

d What would staff on the base not see for many months of the year?

____

e Apart from the ozone layer, what else do scientists at the Halley base study? Name **four** things.

f List **four** points of advice you would give to someone applying for the job in Antarctica.

Writing

7 You recently applied to carry out some summer work in the Antarctic. Write an email to a friend telling them about the job. In your email you should:

- tell your friend about the job and why you wanted to apply
- explain what you had to do to prepare for the interview
- describe what happened at the interview.

Your email should be 150–200 words (Extended) or 100–150 words (Core).

Unit 12: Focus on listening skills

A Vocabulary

1 **Match a verb with a noun to make phrases from Unit 12.**

Verbs	Nouns
provide	suffering
restore	health
alleviate	health
diagnose and treat	illness
prescribe and dispense	illness
perform	medicines
promote	care
prevent	surgery

a ______________

b ______________

c ______________

d ______________

e ______________

f ______________

g ______________

h ______________

2 **Look at this text. Fill in the gaps using some of the verb + noun phrases from Activity A1.**

Nurses care for the sick and injured in hospitals, where they work to **(a)** ______________ and **(b)** ______________. Many people are sent home from the hospital when they still need nursing care, so nurses often **(c)** ______________ in the home that is very similar to the care they give to patients in the hospital. In clinics and health centres in communities that have few doctors, nurses **(d)** ______________, **(e)** ______________ and even **(f)** ______________. Nurses are also increasingly working to **(g)** ______________ and to **(h)** ______________ in all communities.

Adapted from 'Nursing Care for the Sick', by the World Health Organization

3 **Complete the crossword.**

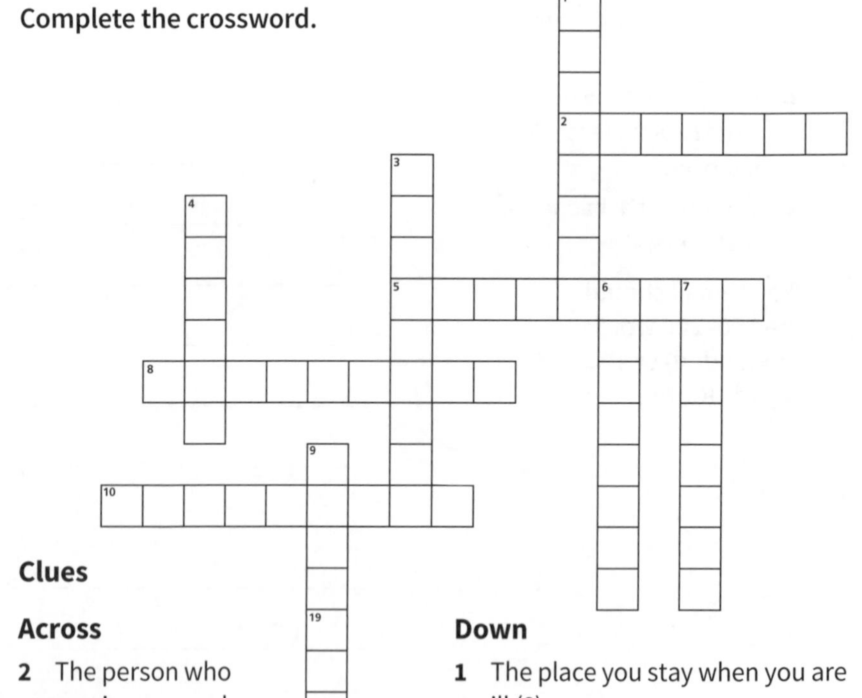

Clues

Across

2 The person who receives care when they are ill (7)

5 A vehicle that carries people when they are ill (9)

8 The care given to someone who is unwell (9)

10 An urgent situation (9)

Down

1 The place you stay when you are ill (8)

3 Trained person who works in 1 Down (9)

4 Damage done to the body (6)

6 An event that can lead to someone being hurt (8)

7 A person who is injured (8)

9 Relating to the treatment of injuries and diseases (7)

4 **What do these acronyms and abbreviations stand for?**

a UCAS ________________________________

b UK ________________________________

c www ________________________________

d IGCSE ________________________________

e A Level ________________________________

f NHS ________________________________

g http ________________________________

h WHO ________________________________

5 **Write four more acronyms or abbreviations that you are familiar with and include their full forms.**

____

____

____

____

6 **There are 16 words/phrases in the word chain below, divided into four categories on topics covered in your Coursebook. Find the words and think of a name for each category. Then complete the table.**

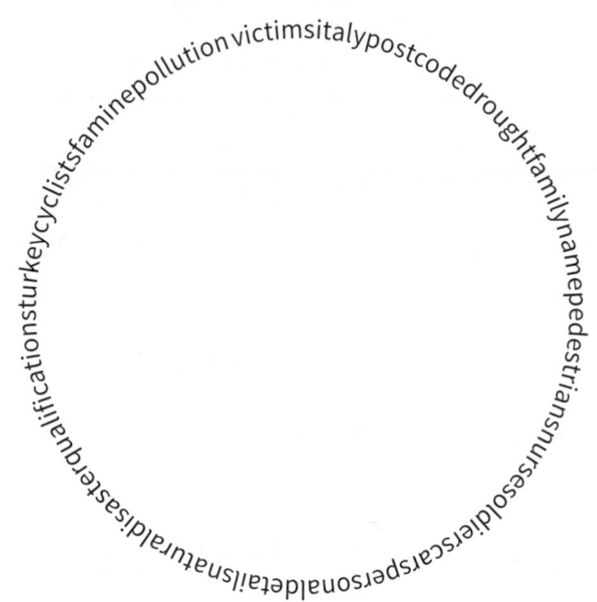

The world			
famine			

B Use of English

1 **Complete this definition for the 'future in the past' using the words in the box.**

will	past	past continuous	future	would

This use of **(a)** ______________ as the past tense of **(b)** ______________ is often referred to as 'future in the past'. It is used to express the idea that in the **(c)** ______________, you thought that something else would happen in the **(d)** ______________. It does not matter if you are correct or not. Both *was/were going to* and the **(e)** ______________ can be used to express the future in the past.

2 **Underline the 'future in the past' phrases in the examples below. Then number the phrase that (1) describes past events and (2) moves forward in time.**

Example: … *the expectation* (1) *was that she would* (2) *marry and start a family …*

a When the doctors heard that Florence Nightingale was going to work with them, they felt threatened.

b The doctors felt threatened when they knew she was soon coming to work with them.

3 Circle the best option to complete each sentence.

a The teacher turned up late just as the students *were about to / would* leave.

b You're home late. I thought we *would go / were going* out for dinner.

c I already told Pietro that when he *would arrive / arrived*, we would go to the cinema.

d Ahmed decided he *would go / will go* to his uncle's house.

e He applied for a different job because he *had planned / was planning* to leave.

f I *would send / was supposed to send* this yesterday, but I forgot.

g All the problems *would / were to* be solved during yesterday's meeting.

h The teacher was absolutely sure her students *would pass / were passing* their exams.

4 Look at the following examples of relative pronouns:

Because of the conflict ***which*** *arose between Florence and her parents …*

Some employers may provide support for staff ***who*** *need to gain further …*

Draw an arrow connecting the relative pronoun with its use.

Relative adverb	Use
who → (arrow to "for people")	for things and animals
which	for expressions of time
that	for expressions of place
when	refers to a reason
whose	for people
where	refers to a possession
why	for people, animals or things

5 Complete the sentences using an appropriate relative pronoun.

a Those are the children ______________ parents did not come to the meeting.

b The place ______________ I met him has since closed down.

c Those are the cars ______________ were involved in the accident last night.

d The reason ______________ we had such a big argument is not important now.

e The person ______________ stole my handbag is kindly asked to hand it back.

f The newspaper ______________ we want to read is always sold out.

g Can you see my cat, ______________ is lying in the sunshine?

h He was walking down the road ______________ he suddenly fell over.

i This is the place ______________ I did my degree, not the other place!

6 Complete the sentences using a relative pronoun and one word for each other gap.

Example: *People* **who** *smoke* **are** *more likely* **to** *develop lung cancer.*

a Children ______________ study ballet ______________ start very young.

b The woman ______________ purse ______________ found on the pavement lives here.

c The computers ______________ belong to the school have never ______________ serviced.

d These roads, ______________ they were built, were ______________ than sufficient for the number of cars.

e The food ______________ was brought to the table ______________ not hot, so I ______________ it back.

f The reason ______________ so many people ______________ the film is because ______________ was excellent.

g The old cinema used to be ______________ the supermarket ______________ now.

C Skills

1 The information in the sentences below comes from one of four texts in the Coursebook:

(i) *Paramedics*

(ii) *Florence Nightingale*

(iii) *ICRC*

(iv) *Traffic*

Write the title of the text next to each sentence.

a Medical facilities for soldiers wounded were criticised. ______________

b Other forms of transport can be used to get to patients. ______________

c The impact upon less developed countries is much greater. ______________

d Many millions have and continue to die due to this development. ______________

e They are normally the first professionals to arrive on the scene. ______________

f She did a three-month training course in Germany. ______________

g They normally work in pairs. ______________

h They are strongly motivated by the nature of their humanitarian work. ______________

i They provide an immediate response. ______________

j An inspiring person who influenced modern healthcare. ______________

k Preference is given to provision of essential goods before healthcare. ______________

l Born in Italy in 1820. ______________

m It provides more than just help in a crisis.

____

n The crisis has reached catastrophic proportions.

____

o They adapt their response to suit the context.

____

p The damage to their health and economic potential will affect them for life.

____

2 Skim the text below and find words that match the following definitions.

a A quality that you have when you are born (adjective, paragraph 1) ______________

b Ideas or methods never used before (adjective, 1) ______________

c Completely (adverb, 2) ______________

d Clearly different from something else (adjective, 3) ______________

e Without having a clear pattern (adjective, 4)

____

Babbling babies have natural rhythm

[1] Babies are born with an innate sense of rhythm that is essential for learning a language, according to a pioneering study of children who learnt 'silent babbling' using sign language. Babbling is common to all babies and was once thought to be merely the result of children learning to move their jaws. But research on the children of deaf parents indicates that a baby babbles to develop its inborn rhythm, which is critical for learning a language. The findings could help children with speech difficulties by providing a better understanding of how infants normally use patterns in the brain's language centres.

[2] Scientists studied babies with normal hearing of profoundly deaf parents and found that, in addition to the random hand movements made by all babies, the infants demonstrated 'silent babbling' using rudimentary signs. By fixing lights to the tips of babies' fingers and analysing their motion, researchers identified non-random movements within normal movements.

[3] The scientists, led by Professor Laura Ann Petitto, of Dartmouth College, New Hampshire, and McGill University, Montreal, write in *Nature*: 'Hearing babies with signing deaf parents make a special kind of movement with their hands, with a specific rhythmic pattern that is distinct from the other hand movements. We figured out that this kind of rhythmic movement was linguistic … it was babbling, but with their hands.'

[4] The scientists compared three babies with normal hearing whose parents were profoundly deaf – and who, therefore, had little exposure to speech – with three babies born to hearing couples who talked to their children. The 'silent babbling' seen in the children of deaf parents was a lower, more rhythmic activity performed closer to the body than the ordinary, random hand movements of infants. Professor Petitto said: 'This dramatic distinction between the two types of hand movements indicates that babies … can make use of the rhythmic patterns underlying human language.' The singsong way many people speak to babies and the patterns of speech in nursery rhymes could be used more effectively in helping handicapped children to speak earlier, the scientists said.

Adapted from an article by Steve Connor in *The Independent*.

3 Read the text more closely, then complete the following sentences. Use your own words as far as possible. You will need to write short phrases, not single words.

a Babbling used to be considered ______________________, but research now shows ______________________.

b In the research, scientists examined ______________________

and observed two things: ______________________ and

______________________ .

c The scientists say that hearing babies with signing deaf parents make

a type of rhythmic movement ______________________, which is

______________________ .

d The babbling of children with deaf parents was ______________________

______________________ .

e Nursery rhymes and the way people speak to babies ______________________

______________________ .

Writing

4 **Read the article about babies and their ability to use a type of sign language with their hands. Write a summary of the results of the research carried out by scientists. Use the notes you made in Activity C3 to help you.**

____

____

____

____

____

____

____

____

____

____

____

____

____

____

____

Unit 13: Focus on reading skills

A Vocabulary

1 Find 12 words from Unit 13 of your Coursebook in the word snake opposite, then write them down.

axisdatasitehorizontalnetworkpercentagecategoryrategraphpopularitychartdiagram

a ______________________ g ______________________

b ______________________ h ______________________

c ______________________ i ______________________

d ______________________ j ______________________

e ______________________ k ______________________

f ______________________ l ______________________

2 Complete the crossword using the words from Activity A1.

Clues

Across

3 The number of times something happens (4)

4 A drawing that shows or explains the parts of something (7)

5 A part of a whole (10)

7 Information in the form of a table (5)

9 Facts or information usually used to calculate (4)

10 A place or location (4)

11 A group of people or things that are similar in some way (8)

Down

1 Positioned from side to side (10)

2 A system of computers and other devices (7)

5 The state of being liked (10)

6 Visual representation of numerical information (5)

8 Straight line that divides something into two parts (4)

3 Decide if the words in italic are nouns or verbs.

a There has been a *reduction* in the number of people failing exams.

____

b The *decline* in the number of applications is very worrying.

____

c If you *drop* this from a great height, it will break. ______________

d To *increase* your grades, you would have to work harder. ______________

e People who *rise* early normally have to use an alarm clock to wake up.

____

f *Dip* your finger in that – it tastes really nice. ______________

g The *fall* of the Roman Empire happened many years ago. ______________

h Due to the *decrease* in sales, we have decided to close the business.

____

i He reached the *peak* of the mountain after one week of hard trekking.

____

4 Below is a list of things that a mobile phone can do. Write in the missing verbs.

a Send or r _ _ _ _ _ _ text messages

b K _ _ _ t _ _ _ _ of appointments

c P _ _ _ games

d S _ _ _ emails

e S _ _ _ _ contact information

f D _ _ _ _ _ _ _ information from the Internet

g W _ _ _ _ TV

h I _ _ _ _ _ _ _ _ other devices

i M _ _ _ task or to-do lists

j U _ _ the built-in calculator

k T _ _ _ pictures

l G _ _ apps

m M _ _ _ videos

n S _ _ reminders

B Use of English

1 **Look at the following sentences. Underline the verb in each sentence, then write them in the correct category in the table.**

a Coconut falls from adult tree.

b Coconut on ground, grows roots.

c New plant grows for eight years.

d From 8–25 years, date palm tree continues to grow, may produce some fruit.

e 25+ years, date palm tree reaches full maturity, produces full load of fruit.

Verbs in the infinitive third person singular	Verb with *to*	Verb with a modal

2 **Rewrite these sentences, correcting the mistakes in the verbs.**

a He told her that he will come.

____

b She said that the moon revolves around the earth.

____

c The teacher and headmaster has come to the classroom.

____

d The price of these jeans are very reasonable.

____

e Neither his father nor mot

____

f I have been listening to this song several times today.

____

g Did you ever taste a cereal called quinoa?

____

h She has already eaten when he got home.

____

C Skills

1 You are going to read an article about a parent's negative perspective on the effect the Internet has on young people. Look at the following seven words from the article, then match each one with a definition from the box.

left alone	very interested in	twelve
leading to success	never ending	
controlled or influenced	being alone	

a dozen ______

b engrossed ______

c abandoned ______

d relentlessly ______

e manipulated ______

f potential ______

g solitude ______

2 Before you read the article, look at the three statements below. Decide if they are true or false. Give a reason for your answers.

a The writer rarely sees a teenager without a computer or smartphone.
True/false

______

b The writer found that teenagers are always positive about their phones.
True/false

______

c Technology has taken the role of the parent.
True/false

______

3 Read the article and underline the words from Activity C1 in the article. Then check if your answers to Activity C2 were correct.

We have abandoned our children to the Internet

A year ago, I walked into my kitchen to find half-a-dozen teenagers there, each one engrossed with their own private screen, in silence. I realised it had been months since I'd seen a teenager without a computer or smartphone in their hand.

What surprised me was the anger of many teenagers who, in turn, felt abandoned by parents whose own eyes were fixed on electronic devices.

Asking a young person to put down their Xbox, switch off their computer or stop looking at their smartphone is like asking a baby to put down its teddy bear. Behind the nursery colours and baby names is a culture that is relentlessly commercial. Each interaction means data – data that is worth a fortune. Our children, manipulated to become exemplary consumers, increasingly admit they do not feel 'in control' of their own internet use.

I am still cautiously hopeful about the potential of the Internet. But it seems that the greatest revolution in communication has been hijacked by commercial values.

Becoming an adult human requires imitation and role models, it takes patience and practice, and it needs both solitude and community. Instead, many of our children have smartphones in the hands that we adults should be holding.

Adapted from www.theguardian.com

4 Answer the following questions based on the article.

a In what way did the writer not find the young people communicating?

______

b How are young people reflecting what their carers do?

______

c Give **two** examples of how computers and smartphones are made to appeal to young people.

______

d What happens each time a person goes online?

______

e What does the writer say has become the dominant feature of the Internet?

____

f Give **four** examples of the roles a computer has taken from that of a parent.

____

____

Writing

5 **Imagine you heard an adult complaining about your use of the Internet and social media. Write an email to a friend in which you repeat what was said. You could use information from this unit, but you are free to include your own ideas as well.**

Write 150–200 words (Extended) or 100–150 words (Core).

Unit 14: Focus on reading and writing skills

A Vocabulary

1 Complete the sentences using the following starter phrases.

It looks/seems like …

It looks/seems as if/though …

It looks/seems …

a ______________________ a car.

b ______________________ so beautiful.

c ______________________ the computer needs fixing.

d ______________________ they are coming early.

e ______________________ silly.

f ______________________ a beautiful day.

2 Write your own sentences using each of the forms in Activity A1.

a It looks like ______________________.

b It seems like ______________________.

c It looks as if ______________________.

d It seems as though ______________________.

e It looks ______________________.

f It seems ______________________.

3 Use the grid to help you work out the words below.

1	2	3	4	5	6	7	8	9	10	11	12	13	14	15	16	17	18	19	20	21	22	23	24	25	26
a	b	c	d	e	f	g	h	i	j	k	l	m	n	o	p	q	r	s	t	u	v	w	x	y	z

Example: *1 2 19 15 18 2 19 = absorbs*

a 3 1 18 22 5 ______________________

b 3 15 21 14 20 5 18 1 3 20 ______________________

c 3 18 21 3 9 1 12 ______________________

d 6 12 15 21 18 9 19 8 ______________________

e 6 18 1 7 9 12 5 ______________________

f 8 21 12 12 19 ______________________

g 19 8 18 9 14 11 9 14 7 ______________________

h 19 11 9 18 20 ______________________

i 22 5 19 19 5 12 ______________________

B Use of English

1 Look at these phrases with verbs in the passive:

Nowadays, every cyclonic disturbance is detected by satellite.

At that time, Antarctica did not exist as a separate continent, but was connected to …

Today, Antarctica is covered by polar ice.

Decide if the following information about the passive is true or false

a The passive is formed with the verb *to be* + past participle. True/false

b *Am*, *is* and *are* are forms of the verb *to be*. True/false

c The passive voice focuses more on the action of a sentence. True/false

d The passive is often used in formal and technical English. True/false

e In the passive, it is not always necessary to know who does the action. True/false

f There are no irregular verb forms in the past participle. True/false

2 Change the following sentences into the passive.

Example: *People expect him to be the next Head of Science.*
He is expected to be the next Head of Science.

a Firemen have reported that the fire is out of control.

____

b Some people think that saving money is better than spending it.

____

c The municipality built that ugly modern building for thousands of euros.

____

d Countries around the world celebrate different public holidays.

____

e NASA has sent up another satellite for the weather.

____

f People who loved the book *The Lord of the Rings* also enjoyed the film.

____

3 Look at these phrases showing comparisons:

… supported a far wider and more abundant plant and animal life than …

… making it the 'quietest' continent in terms of earthquake movement.

Choose two texts from Unit 14 of the Coursebook and find four more phrases or sentences where comparisons are made. Write them below.

a ______________________________

b ______________________________

c ______________________________

d ______________________________

C Skills

1 You are going to read a report written by young people. In this report, people were asked: *What does climate change mean to young people?* Write your answers in note form for each of the questions a–d below.

a Do you think climate change will impact your life in any way?

____

b In what ways are you aware of changes to the climate (this could be in your country or abroad)?

____

c Which countries in the world have been worst affected?

____

d Give examples of what climate change is.

____

2 The report claims: *Climate change is a global problem and is set to hit the youngest hardest, particularly in developing states.* Decide if the following statements about climate change are true or false.

a Climate change has affected most countries. True/false

b Governments always support young peoples' efforts to help the environment. True/false

c Developing countries are the worst affected because they have fewer resources. True/false

d There is little effort and change being made by many countries to improve the situation. True/false

3 Skim the text on page 82 and match each country to a section (a–d). Give two reasons (i and ii) for each choice.

India	France	Peru	Rwanda

a *France.*

i) *Because he uses the French words:* modèle social.

ii) ______________________________

b ______________________________

i) ______________________________

ii) ______________________________

c ______________________________

i) ______________________________

ii) ______________________________

d ______________________________

i) ______________________________

ii) ______________________________

[a] Antoine Ebel, 22, ________________

The report doesn't change much. It confirms what we already knew – human activities have a catastrophic influence on our climate. Whether we are 90% or 95% certain of that is mostly irrelevant.

Our duty as young people is to highlight the solutions, imagining, describing and starting to build a climate-friendly world that people will want to live in – demonstrating that climate change is also a chance to start things fresh, rethink and rebuild our societies on more solid and sustainable bases.

I also think that we need to realise, as a country, that climate change is affecting us too. It's not just about us being 'charitable' to small islands and polar bears when we reduce our emissions; we're also keeping our *modèle social* alive.

[b] Alexandra Gavilano, 24, ________________

In . . . , climate change is noticeable by various changes in the local weather. In the highlands of the Andean mountains, heavy rains called *huaico* by the local people, with never-seen-before tennis-ball-sized hailstones, destroy the houses and infrastructure of the small towns.

But the rain doesn't stay in the mountains. In February, the city of Trujillo was partially flooded, shutting down the electricity and infrastructure in parts of the city. Parts of the Chan Chan sandstone ruins were destroyed. Rain now falls in an area that was distinct for centuries for its dry and hot weather.

It's interesting that a lot of youngsters in . . . , either in universities or doing art on the street, want to make a change, but feel stopped by the national government, which has shown heavy threats with military forces against people standing up against governmental interests.

[d] Neeshad V. S., 26, ________________

The implications of the report are of utmost importance to . . . as well as the rest of the world.

Climate change impacts can be seen on various sectors across Asia, including . . . . The frequency of more intense rainfall events in many parts of Asia has increased, causing severe floods, landslides, debris and mud flows, while the numbers of rainy days have decreased.

With over 400 LEED-certified buildings and many states adopting the Energy Conservation Building Code (ECBC), . . . continues to make strides in reducing its carbon emissions. . . . can also create a low-carbon development path by shifting to clean energy. Progress made to achieve . . .'s National Solar Mission is one example of the way forward, though much more needs to be done to continue . . .'s rapid growth sustainably.

This undeniable evidence of human-caused warming and the catastrophic results of inaction should spur the world's largest and oldest democracies into seizing this urgent opportunity for cooperation.

[e] Yves Tuyishime, 27, ________________

Africa is one of the most vulnerable continents to climate change and has lower adaptive capacity. Most African economies depend on agriculture and changing weather threatens African agriculture.

It is obvious that Africa is not being affected by emissions 'made in Africa'. Africa's share of global emissions is relatively small compared to emissions from the developed world.

No matter how much mitigation effort Africa puts in, it remains insignificant unless industrialised countries do something. Therefore, we are calling for action by developed countries.

Adapted from www.rtcc.org

4 Look back at the statements in Activity C2. Scan the text to find out whether you made the correct decisions. Give reasons for your answers.

a ______________________________

b ______________________________

c ______________________________

d ______________________________

5 Answer these questions about the text.

a Why does Antoine give the two figures? What is he trying to stress?

____

b What is Antoine referring to with the expression *modèle social*?

____

c What does Alexandra say about the area that was once *distinct*?

____

d Why are heavy threats and military force used against the young people in Peru?

____

e What has reduced in Asia?

____

f Who does Neeshad suggest should encourage other countries to work together?

____

g Why does Yves think Africa improving its environment will not have much world impact?

____

h What unwittingly is being imported into Africa and having an impact on its economy?

____

6 Answer this exam-style question.

You have been asked by your teacher to make a presentation to students entitled: *What does climate change mean to young people in my country?* You need to make notes in order to prepare. Make your notes under each heading.

Main environmental issues in my country

-
-

How the environment has changed in my country

-
-

What efforts (if any) are being made to improve the environment in my country?

-
-

Other

-
-
-

Writing

7 Imagine that you have given your presentation. Now your teacher has asked you to follow this up with a summary for students. Look at your notes to help you write your summary.

Your summary should be about 70 words long (and no more than 80 words long). You should use your own words as far as possible.

Unit 15: Focus on writing skills

A Vocabulary

1 Join the parts of the words or phrases together to make words from Unit 15. Write the complete words/phrases below.

ef…y	clean-	-ented	out-	-ficienc-
-tering la-	lit- -w	exe-	*-ndals*	-ce peri-
con…uently	desi…d	-liness	-gnate-	-seq-
-cuted	gra- -od	-lawed	*va-*	implem-

Example: *vandals*

a ______________________________

b ______________________________

c ______________________________

d ______________________________

e ______________________________

f ______________________________

g ______________________________

h ______________________________

i ______________________________

2 Use the words and phrases from Activity A1 to complete the following sentences.

Example: Vandals *had broken into the school at night and destroyed the gym.*

a ____________ is a very important part of learning about personal hygiene.

b They arrived late and ____________ missed the beginning of the film.

c She was entitled to a ____________ because of her family issues.

d The corporation ____________ a series of financial deals.

e There is a ____________ in Singapore that has harsh penalties.

f She impressively completed the task with great ____________ .

g Funds were specifically ____________ to renovate the ancient sites.

h That treatment has been ______________ by the government because of the side effects.

i They ______________ their chores quickly so they could go out.

3 Match the phrases and then copy and rewrite the complete sentence below. There may be more than one possible match for some of the phrases.

~~As a result, in January 1992, …~~	… everybody used to park on the double yellow line.
In addition to this cost …	… was introduced there was much opposition to it.
In January 2014, …	… smoking was banned in all public places.
In March 2010, …	… were the taxes, which were 17.3%.
Prior to the introduction of the law, …	~~… they decided to implement the law.~~
When the ban …	… there were storms which destroyed many homes.

Example: *As a result, in January 1992, they decided to implement the law.*

a ______________________________

b ______________________________

c ______________________________

d ______________________________

e ______________________________

B Use of English

1 Are the following statements about the words *affect* and *effect* true or false?

a If you are talking about a result then you should use the word *effect*. True/false

b The word *effect* can come before the following: *on*, *of*, *with*, *from*, *into*. True/false

c The word *affect* means to produce a change in something. True/false

d *Affect* can be used as a noun and a verb. True/false

e *Affect* is a verb and *effect* is a noun. True/false

2 Complete the sentences using either *affect* or *effect*.

a The teacher said that this test would have no ______________ on our final grade.

b I did not expect the film to ______________ me in the way it did.

c I did not let his anger _____________ me.

d The _____________ of the light in the room is very pleasing.

e His absences from school are starting to _____________ his grades.

f The new school regulations had the desired _____________ .

3 Complete the table with the correct word forms. You may not be able to fill in all the gaps.

Adjective	Noun	Verb
dental		
	freshener	
	hungry	
		harm
digestive		
	science/scientist	
		benefit
cognitive		
	sweetener/sweet	
		satisfy

4 Complete the information using an appropriate word from the table in Activity B3.

a Dr Maria Bealing, a _____________ expert.

b The Greeks used bark from mastic trees as a breath _____________ .

c The brain is alerted that the _____________ process is about to begin, but is chewing gum _____________ to the body?

d _____________ studies have not successfully proven that gum can stave off _____________ .

e So are there any _____________ in gum chewing?

f Recent studies have shown that chewing gum during a task can increase _____________ function.

g The minty or fruity flavour of the gum will _____________ your breath and _____________ a sweet tooth.

C Skills

1 You are going to read an article called *Should cooking be taught at school?* First, answer the following questions in your notebook.

a Can you cook? If yes, what can you cook? If no, would you like to learn? Why, or why not?

b Do you think that cookery should be taught at school? Why, or why not?

c If you were to learn to cook at school, what exactly do you think you should learn – for example how to make coffee, the nutritional value of food?

d What other subjects do you think should be taught at your school? List at least two.

2 Look at the following points. Decide if they are in favour of cookery classes at school or not in favour. Put a tick or a cross in the box.

a It is one of the basic skills in life and everyone should be taught it. ☐

b It is not necessary to learn because somebody in the home already has these skills. ☐

c There are much more important things to learn. ☐

d Food is not made like that nowadays, so what's the point in learning it? ☐

e It should be part of learning about a healthy lifestyle. ☐

f I'm just not interested. ☐

3 Look at these phrases from the text. Write the numeral for the phrase to fill in the gaps in the article.

(i) … for the best chef …

(ii) … a healthy lifestyle as by studying nutrition, …

(iii) … merely a female domain, as some of …

(iv) … and unable to take care of themselves.

(v) Thus, it is important for students …

(vi) … could develop in an area not exposed to before.

Should cooking be taught at school?
by Chan Chi Man, Cathy

Children nowadays are often blamed for being spoiled **(a)** ______________ . A compulsory home economics course is an effective method to address this problem.

By learning basic skills like cooking, cleaning and money management, students can learn how to take care of themselves. We know that when parents become older or die, children need to live independently and look after their own families. **(b)** ______________ to come to grips with these important skills early in life. To make sure that all students – regardless of gender and age – learn these skills, a compulsory home economics class is a must.

This can also help them develop **(c)**______________ they are more likely to have a balanced diet instead of consuming fast food and ready-made meals, which contain a lot of fat, salt and sugar.

On top of that, children should have more opportunities to develop different interests. Not everybody wants to study Mathematics and Physics, for example. So, students who are not academically or scientifically inclined **(d)** ______________ .

There is increasingly a general acceptance that 'food' and 'cookery' have now become buzz words and there is a lot of excitement about the industry and the opportunities there. Catering or cookery is no longer seen as **(e)**______________ the top international chefs are actually men. It is a highly competitive industry and one with vast opportunities. Recent media coverage has had a large impact on this, where 'cooking' is no longer associated with gender and just the home. Programmes covering all aspects of food hygiene, the catering industry and competitions **(f)** ______________ are shown every day on the television

So why not make our home economics class compulsory?

Adapted from www.scmp.com

Writing

4 Answer this exam-style question.

You have been informed that you are to start cookery classes at your school. Write an email or letter to a friend, telling them about your feelings on this.

In your email or letter, you should:

- tell your friend why cookery classes are being started
- describe what the lessons will involve
- explain how you feel about the decision.

Your email or letter should be 150–200 words (Extended) or 100–150 words (Core). Do not write an address.

The pictures on the left may give you some ideas and you should try to include some ideas of your own.

You will receive up to 10 (Extended)/7 (Core) marks for the content of your letter and up to 9 (Extended)/6 (Core) marks for the style and accuracy of your language.

Unit 16: Focus on speaking skills

A Vocabulary

1 What is the difference in meaning between the pairs of words opposite? Use paper or digital reference sources to help you write your answers.

Example: *newspaper / magazine*
A newspaper usually comes out every day and normally covers all types of news. A magazine usually deals with specific areas and is normally weekly or monthly.

a career / job

____

____

b picture / photograph

____

____

c industry / factory

____

____

d shy / nervous

____

____

e confident / brave

____

____

2 Match these definitions to five words from Activity A1.

a opposite in meaning to **c** ______________________________

____

b a job for a lifetime ______________________________

____

c could mean 'embarrassed' ______________________________

____

d picture taken with a camera ______________________________

____

e place where things are produced ______________________________

____

3 **Use a dictionary to find out what the words below mean, then write a brief explanation for each one.**

a catwalk

____

b chic

____

c accessories

____

d haute couture

____

e designer wear

____

f look

____

g fashionista

____

4 **Complete the sentences using the words from Activity A3.**

a She likes to buy lots of ______________ to make her clothes more interesting.

b Our school uniform has tried to imitate the new ______________ , but has failed miserably.

c He fell off the ______________ when they were rehearsing for the show.

d She looked very ______________ in her new outfit.

e France and Italy are major locations in Europe for ______________ .

f He is such a ______________ that he spends all his salary on a new wardrobe every month.

g Some people cannot tell the difference between ______________ and that from a shop.

5 **How many words can you make in three minutes from the given letters? You can only use a letter once in a word. Each letter is worth one point.**

Example: *pan = 3 points*

spar = 4 points

C	N	D	F
A	P	H	L
R	A	S	P
N	B	R	M

B Use of English

1 Look at how *whether ... or* is used in these sentences:

*... decide **whether** the following statements are true **or** false.*

***Whether** you go in my car **or** in hers, you are going to be late.*

Write four sentences using *whether ... or ...*

a ______________________________

b ______________________________

c ______________________________

d ______________________________

2 Match the 'signpost' words in the box to the sentences below.

although	even though	despite	in spite of

a We use a noun or a pronoun after this. ______________

b The only difference between them is the word *of.* ______________

c After this we use a subject and a verb. ______________

d We can use these with a subject and a verb if we include the expression *the fact that.* ______________

e This is a slightly stronger form of *although.* ______________

3 Complete the sentences using *although*, *even though*, *despite* or *in spite of.* Sometimes, more than one option is possible.

a ______________ we are a small school, we have a very good track record for examination results.

b ______________ all the difficulties, the performance started on time.

c ______________ we were warned about going to see the film, we still went.

d ______________ his lack of experience, he had a successful career.

e ______________ I was tired, I could not sleep.

f I like my school, ______________ the distance from my home.

g I walked home, ______________ the fact that my legs were tired.

h ______________ we went to school together every day, we were not close friends.

i ______________ his injury, he swims every day.

4 **Look at the following sentences. Three different tenses have been used. Write the tense next to the sentence.**

a The clothing industry is backward. ______________

b The first Jeane Company jeans were sold in 1874. ______________

c One day, all clothes will contain micro-computers. ______________

5 **Look at the questions below. Identify each of the tenses, then answer the question using the same tense.**

Example: *What do you do every day? Present simple.*
I go to school.

a What did you do yesterday? ______________

____

b What will you do tomorrow if it rains? ______________

____

c What are you doing right now? ______________

____

d What were you doing at this time yesterday? ______________

____

e What will you be doing at this time tomorrow? ______________

____

f What have you done today? ______________

____

g What had you done before he arrived? ______________

____

h What will you have done by ten o'clock this morning? ______________

____

i What have you been doing this morning? ______________

____

C Skills

1 How much can you remember about bespoke shoes from Unit 16? Write down at least five things.

a ______________________________

b ______________________________

c ______________________________

d ______________________________

e ______________________________

2 Connect phrases from Column A to Column B.

A	B
Along with the shoe, …	… they are called 'bespoke shoes'.
Bespoke shoes are made in exactly the same way as they were 100 years ago, …	… that still make traditional bespoke men's shoes.
Next, a wooden model of your foot is made, …	… as the technology is completely unchanged.
The designs, like the process, …	… one thing that is being built is the ego of the client.
The idea of a platform heel, a multicoloured shoe or a trainer …	… called a 'last'.
There are now only five companies in London …	… have remained unchanged for a century.
When shoes are made to fit your feet and nobody else's, …	… is unknown to the maker of the bespoke shoe, and the client.

3 Complete the phrases using words from the box.

century	client	model	premises	sheet	statement

a Bespoke shoes make a ______________ .

b The ______________ for these London companies are small.

c It still takes three months to make the first pair of shoes for a ______________ .

d You put your foot on a ______________ of paper.

e Next, a wooden ______________ of your foot is made.

f The designs have remained unchanged for a ______________ .

Writing

4 **Imagine that you recently spoke to your teacher to talk about your future and career. Write an email or letter to a friend, telling them what you discussed. In your email or letter you should:**

- describe who you spoke to and some of the questions you were asked
- explain what you learned and what ideas were given to you
- give your opinion about how you think you can accomplish what the teacher suggested.

Your email or letter should be 150–200 words (Extended) or 100–150 words (Core).

Acknowledgements

The author and publishers are grateful for the permissions granted to reproduce texts in either the original or adapted form. While every effort has been made, it has not always been possible to identify the sources of the all materials used, or to trace all copyright holders. If any omissions are brought to our notice, we will be happy to include the appropriate acknowledgements on reprinting.

pp. 16 and 17 adapted from 'Beyond Malala: six teenagers changing the world' by Jonathan Kaiman in Beijing, Amanda Holpuch in New York, David Smith in Johannesburg, Jonathan Watts in Rio de Janeiro, and Alexandra Topping, www.theguardian.com, 18 October 2013, © Guardian News and Media Ltd 2013. Reprinted by permission; p. 33 adapted from 'Video Game Addiction. Physical Consequences of Gaming Addiction' from www.video-game-addiction.org. Reprinted by permission of CRC Health; p. 43 this article uses material from the Wikipedia article http://en.wikipedia.org/wiki/Dirty_Jobs, which is released under the http://creativecommons.org/licenses/by-sa/3.0, Creative Commons Attribution-Share-Alike License 3.0; p. 54 adapted from an article from www.moscowtimes.ru, 23 January 2004. Reprinted by permission; pp. 60–61 adapted from 'Felix Baumgartner: watch the jump', 14 October 2012, www.telegraph.co.uk © Telegraph Media Group Limited 2012. Reprinted by permission; p. 66 adapted from 'It's the coldest, most isolated continent on earth. Why would anyone want to work there?' by Tania Branigan, 6 August 2001, *The Guardian* © Guardian News and Media Ltd 2001. Reprinted by permission; p. 68 adapted extract from 'Nursing Care for the Sick' from 'A Guide for Nurses Working in Small Rural Hospitals' Second Edition, by World Health Organization Regional Office for the Western Pacific, Manila, Philippines 2003. Reprinted by permission; p. 72 adapted from an article by Steve Connor from *The Independent* (www.independent.co.uk), 6 September 2001. Reprinted by permission; p. 77 adapted from 'We have abandoned our children to the internet' by Beeban Kidron, *The Guardian*, 13 September 2013 © Guardian News and Media Ltd 2013. Reprinted by permission; p. 82 adapted from 'What does climate change mean to young people?' 14 October 2013. Reprinted by permission of RTCC (Responding to Climate Change); p. 88 adapted from www.scmp.com/article/1002382/should-cooking-be-taught-school, by Chan Chi Man, Cathy. reprinted by permission.

Picture credits

p. 53 (t) Getty Images; p. 53 (b) Kaliva/Shutterstock; p. 59 (l) Getty Images; p. 59 (r) ABACA/ABACA/Press Association Images.

Produced for Cambridge University Press by
White-Thomson Publishing
+44 (0)843 208 7460
www.wtpub.co.uk

Project editor: Sonya Newland
Designer: Clare Nicholas
Illustrator: Steve Evans